Debbie Mumm®
Quilts
SANTA'S SCRAPBOOK

Elves and teapots, crazy quilts and leaping deer
Preserve the holiday spirit all through the year!

DEBBIE MUMM
MUMM'S THE WORD®

DEAR FRIENDS,

The holidays are my favorite time of year! I love everything about the season—decorating my home, buying and creating gifts for everyone I love, the music, the magic, the cookies! I've tried to capture that magical feeling of the Christmas season in this beautiful new book.

Playful elves introduce each project and whimsical artwork is woven throughout the pages of Santa's Scrapbook. Each page looks like it came straight from Santa's desk at #1 North Pole Lane. Mrs. Claus plays her part with a whole chapter of wonderful quilt projects including a Christmas Tea Wall Quilt, Sweet Treats Apron, Gingerbread Garland, and Christmas Ribbon Table Quilt. Mrs. Claus' Christmas project is a sumptuous crazy quilt featuring leftover velvets from Santa's suits.

Graceful deer leap across our bed-size quilt and an intricate snowflake wallhanging captures all the magic of a winter snowfall. Ella and Elwood Elf join Santa in the workshop as they make a shelf full of vintage toys and a Toyland Crib Quilt. Santa's toolbox even receives attention with a delightful paint treatment.

The miracle of Christmas night comes to life with our Starry Night Tree Skirt and To All A Good Night Mantel Cover. Turned-up Toes Stockings, Everything Elfish Miniature Tree, and other delightful projects are perfect to decorate your home or give as gifts.

The holidays wouldn't be complete without lots of photos and reminders of this most special of times. We dress up Santa's scrapbook with an embroidered crazy quilt cover and show you how to create your own personalized scrapbook pages.

Make new memories and establish new holiday traditions by creating these beautiful hand-crafted projects. Or just take a few minutes for yourself during this busy time of year to enjoy the beautiful photos and delightful artwork in your book. I hope it will bring a smile to your face and beautiful projects to your home.

With Love and Joy,

Debbie Mumm

Table of Contents

SANTA'S WORKSHOP

NICE

Bobby
Heather
Georgie
Mya
Debbie
Steven
Nancy
Thomas
Cyndi
Robin
Maggie
Lou
Brenda
...dy
...-Jin
...eter
Sherry
Kaleb
Colton
Justin
Hillary
Jacob

Santa's Toolbox

Months before
Christmas Santa
and the elves
Are busy in the workshop filling
the shelves,
Toys must be made and stockings filled
So that Christmas dreams can soon
be fulfilled.

Toyland Crib Quilt

Toyland Crib Quilt
Finished size: 51" x 68"
Photo Page 9

The timeless tradition of Christmas toys is celebrated in this adorable quilt that is perfect for the nursery! Time-honored toys are machine appliquéd on this easy-to-piece crib or lap size quilt. Read all instructions before beginning and use ¼"-wide seams throughout.

Fabric Requirements

Background - 1⅙ yards
Block Background - 1¼ yards
Block Borders
  red - ⅜ yard (total of
    assorted reds)
  green - ⅜ yard (total of
    assorted greens)
Appliquéd Toys - Assorted
  scraps
Accent Border - ⅜ yard
Outside Border - ¾ yard
Binding - ⅝ yard
Backing - 3½ yards
Batting - 59" x 76" piece
Lightweight fusible web
  1 yard
Fabric Stabilizer - 1 yard

Cutting the Strips and Pieces

Before you begin, read Cutting the Strips and Pieces on page 108.

	FIRST CUT		SECOND CUT	
	Number of Strips or Pieces	Dimensions	Number of Pieces	Dimensions
BACK-GROUND	1	18¼" x 42"	2	18¼" squares (cut twice diagonally)
	1	12¼" x 42"	2	12¼" squares (cut once diagonally)
	1	8½" x 42"	2	8½" squares
BLOCK BACK-GROUND	4	8½" x 42"	6	8½" x 14½"
			12	3½" x 8½"
	1	3½" x 42"	4	3½" squares
	2	2½" x 42"	17	2½" squares
BORDERS				
RED BLOCK BORDER	7	1½" x 42"	12	1½" x 8½"
			17	1½" x 4½"
			17	1½" x 2½"
GREEN BLOCK BORDER	7	1½" x 42"	12	1½" x 8½"
			17	1½" x 4½"
			17	1½" x 2½"
ACCENT BORDER	5	1½" x 42"		
	2	1½" x 42"	8	1½" x 5½"
			8	1½" x 3½"
OUTSIDE BORDER	5	4½" x 42"		
BINDING	7	2¾" x 42"		

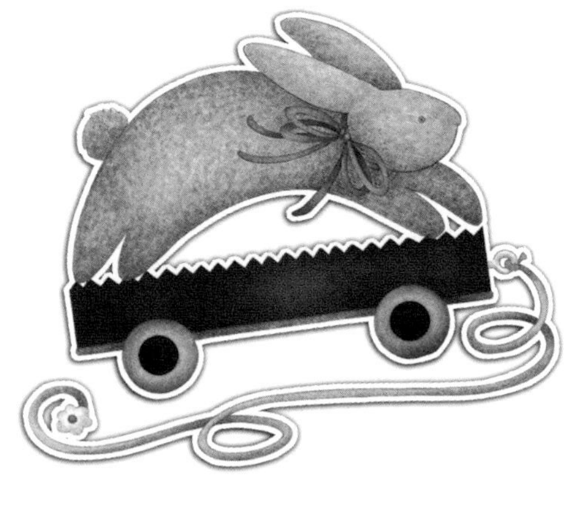

Making the Center

1. Sew one 8½" x 14½" block background piece between two 1½" x 8½" red block border pieces. Press. Repeat to make three.

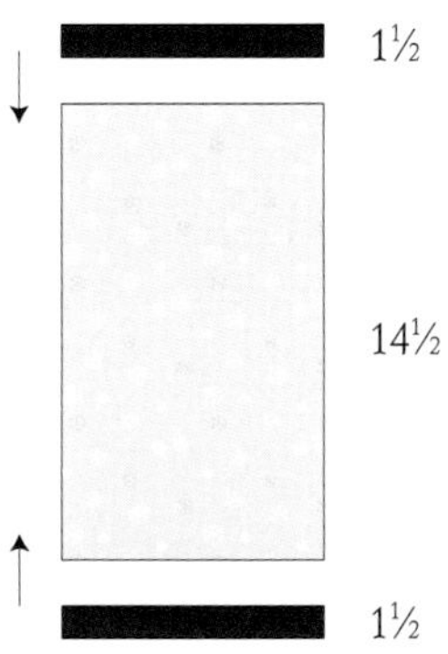

Make 3

2. Sew one 8½" background square between two units from step 1. Press. Make one.

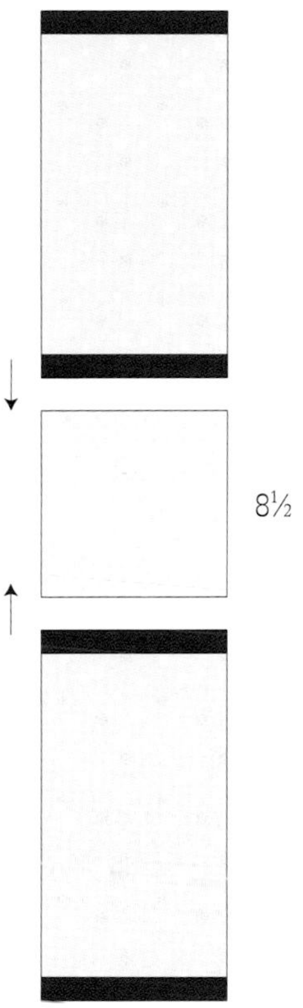

3. Using 1½" x 8½" green block border pieces, remaining 8½" x 14½" block background pieces, and 8½" background square, repeat steps 1 and 2.

4. Sew seventeen 2½" block background squares between seventeen green and seventeen red 1½" x 2½" block border pieces. Press. Add seventeen red and seventeen green 1½" x 4½" block border pieces to sides. Press.

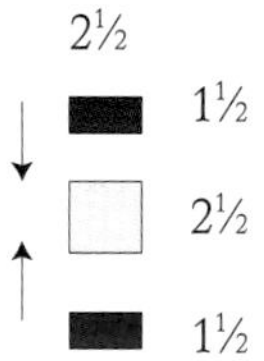

Make 17

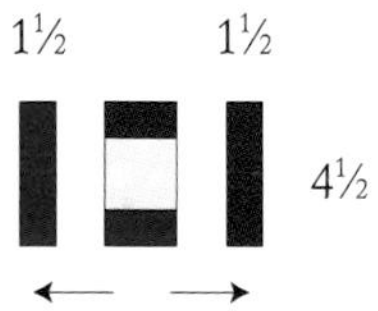

Make 17

5. Sew six 1½" x 8½" red block border pieces to the side of six 3½" x 8½" block background pieces. Press. Repeat to sew six 1½" x 8½" green block border pieces to the side of the remaining six block background pieces. Press.

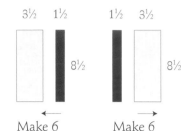

Make 6   Make 6

6. Sew five red-sided units and three green-sided units from step 5 between sixteen units from step 4, taking care to match colors correctly. Press.

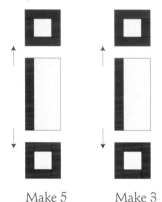

Make 5   Make 3

7. Sew one red-sided unit from step 6 to side of one red border unit from step 1 to make Row 1. Sew one green-sided unit from step 6 to side of one green border unit from step 3 to make Row 5.

Row 1   Row 5

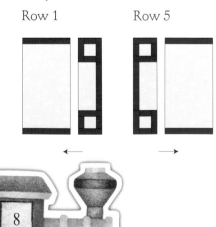

8. Sew remaining red border unit from step 5 between two green-sided units from step 6. Sew two green border units from step 5 between two red-sided units from step 6 and remaining unit from step 4. Sew remaining green border unit from step 5 between two red border units from step 6.

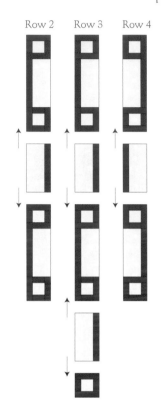

Row 2   Row 3   Row 4

9. Sew unit from step 3 to Row 2 in step 8. Sew unit from step 2 to Row 4 from step 8. Press.

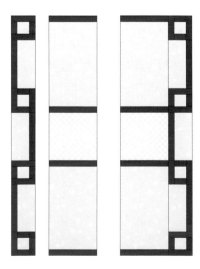

10. Referring to diagram for placement, assemble rows 1, 2, 3, 4, and 5, adding 18¼" background setting triangles as shown. Press.

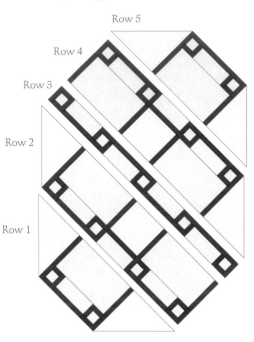

Row 5
Row 4
Row 3
Row 2
Row 1

11. Referring to layout page 6, add four 12¼" background corner triangles to each corner. Press.

Adding the Borders

1. Measure quilt width and length.

2. Sew two 1½" x 42" accent border strips lengthwise to two 4½" x 42" outside border strips. Press. Cut strips to width measurement. Sew these border sections to the top and bottom of quilt. Press.

3. Cut one 1½" x 42" accent border strip and one 4½" x 42" outside border strip in half crosswise. Sew halves to remaining two accent borders and outside border strips. Cut strips to length measurement from step 1.

4. Sew an accent border strip to each outside border strip from step 3. Press.

8

5. To make corner squares, sew four 3½" block background squares between eight 1½" x 3½" accent border pieces. Press. Repeat to add 1½" x 5½" accent border strips to sides. Press.

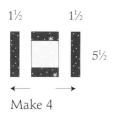

1½   1½

5½

Make 4

6. Referring to Quilt Layout on page 6, sew two border units from step 4 between four corner squares from step 5. Press and sew to sides of quilt.

Appliquéd Toys

1. Refer to Quick-Fuse Appliqué directions on page 109. Trace appliqué patterns from pages 10-15 onto paper side of fusible web. Quick fuse to block centers, referring to color photo below for placement. All appliqué patterns for this quilt have been reversed for use with the quick-fuse technique. If another appliqué technique is used, you may need to alter the pattern.

2. Finish edges using a machine blanket, satin, or small zigzag stitch. If desired, use tear-away stabilizer on wrong side of block for an even stitch.

Layering and Finishing

1. Arrange and baste backing, batting, and top together, referring to Layering the Quilt directions on page 110.

2. Machine or hand quilt as desired.

3. Sew four 2¾" x 42" binding strips together in pairs. Cut one binding strip in half lengthwise and sew half to each of two remaining binding strips. Using the four binding pieces, refer to Binding the Quilt directions on page 111 to finish.

Tracing Line _____

Tracing Line _ _ _ _ _ _ _ _ _ _ _ _
(will be hidden behind other fabrics)

Appliqué pattern is reversed for
use with quick-fuse technique.

Tracing Line _____

Tracing Line - - - - - - - - - - - - - -
(will be hidden behind other fabrics)

*Appliqué pattern is reversed for
use with quick-fuse technique.*

11

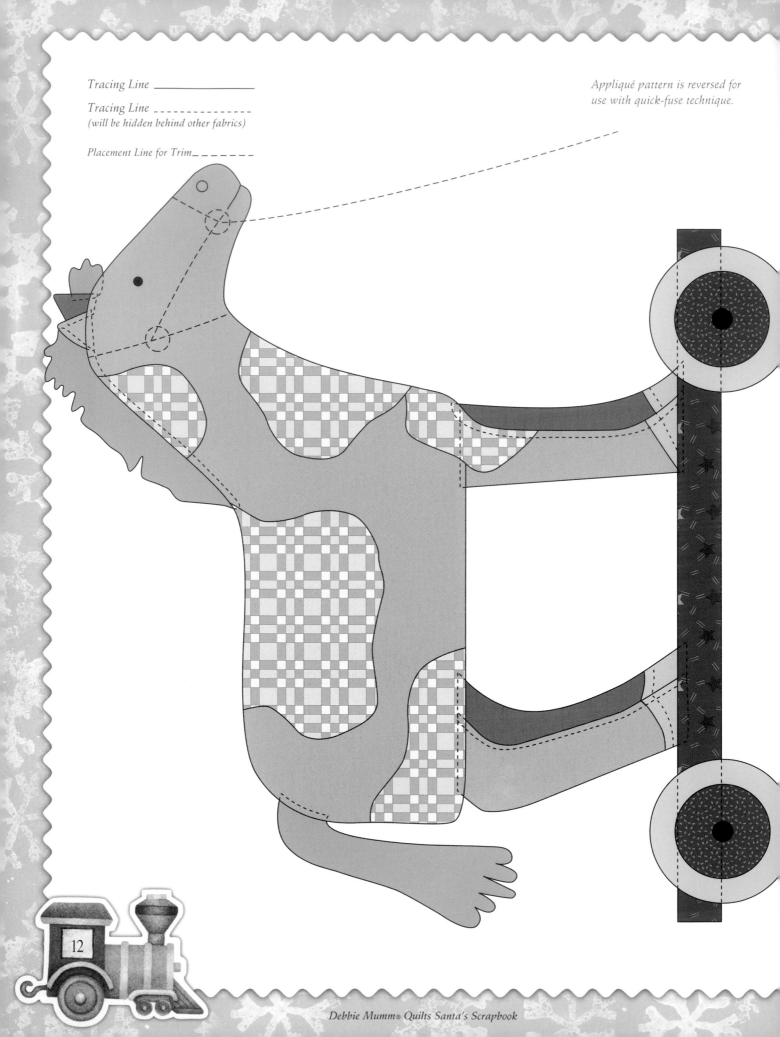

Tracing Line _____

Tracing Line _ _ _ _ _ _ _ _ _ _
(will be hidden behind other fabrics)

Placement Line for Trim _ _ _ _ _

Appliqué pattern is reversed for
use with quick-fuse technique.

12

Tracing Line _____

Tracing Line _ _ _ _ _ _ _ _ _ _
(will be hidden behind other fabrics)

Appliqué pattern is reversed for use with quick-fuse technique.

13

Tracing Line _____

Tracing Line - - - - - - - - - - - -
(will be hidden behind other fabrics)

Appliqué pattern is reversed for
use with quick-fuse technique.

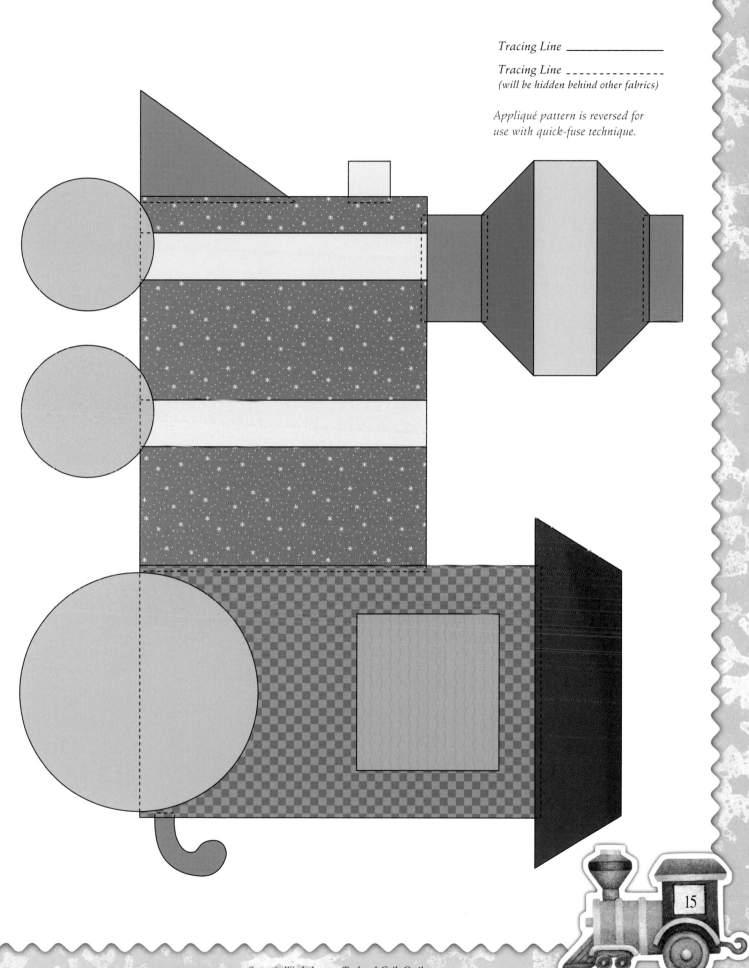

Tracing Line _____

Tracing Line - - - - - - - - - - - - -
(will be hidden behind other fabrics)

*Appliqué pattern is reversed for
use with quick-fuse technique.*

15

All I Want for Christmas Wall Quilt

All I Want for Christmas Wall Quilt

Finished size: 50¹/₂" x 21"
Photo page 21

The nostalgia of Christmases past is captured in this winsome
wall quilt. Books and blocks are pieced into the background while
quick-fused toys make this project fast and easy.
Read all instructions before beginning
and use ¹/₄"-wide seams throughout.

Fabric Requirements

Background - ³/₄ yard
Shelf - Light brown - ¹/₈ yard
  Medium brown - ¹/₆ yard
  Dark brown - scraps
Books - Scraps - Assorted lights,
  mediums, and darks in blue,
  gold, green, tan, red
Boxes - Assorted light, medium,
  and dark scraps
Blocks - Assorted light,
  medium, and dark scraps
Toyland Appliqués - Assorted
  colorful scraps
Accent Border - ¹/₄ yard
Outside Border - ¹/₂ yard
Binding - ¹/₂ yard
Backing - 1²/₃ yards
Batting - 55" x 25" piece
Heavyweight fusible web
  1 yard

16

Cutting the Strips and Pieces

Before you begin, read Cutting the Strips and Pieces on page 108.

	FIRST CUT		SECOND CUT	
	Number of Strips or Pieces	Dimensions	Number of Strips or Pieces	Dimensions
FABRIC A BACK-GROUND	1	10" x 42"	2 1 1	10" x 10½" 8½" x 10" 6½" x 8½"
	2	2½" x 42"	1 1 1	2½" x 36½" 2½" x 6½" 2½" square
	1	1½" x 42"	1 3 8	1½" x 3½" 1½" x 2½" 1½" squares
	1	6½" x 6"		
	1	2" x 4½"		
FABRIC B SHELF LIGHT	2	1½" x 42"	1 1 2	1½" x 24½" 1½" x 20½" 1½" squares
FABRIC C SHELF MEDIUM	1	2½" x 42"	1 1 1 1	2½" x 10½" 2½" x 9½" 2½" x 7½" 2½" square
	1	1½" x 42"	2 4	1½" x 3½" 1½" squares
FABRIC D SHELF DARK	4	1½" squares		
BORDERS				
ACCENT BORDER	4	1¼" x 42"		
OUTSIDE BORDER	5	2½" x 42"		
BINDING	5	2¾" x 42"		

Making the Background

You will be making many quick corner triangles to piece the bookshelf and the items on it. Refer to Quick Corner Triangle Instructions on page 108 to complete the triangle units. The quilt has been divided into sections to make cutting and sewing instructions easy to follow. See page 21 to preview section division.

Section One

1. Make a quick corner triangle unit by sewing one 2½" Fabric A square to the end of one 2½" x 10½" Fabric C piece.

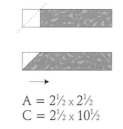

A = 2½ x 2½
C = 2½ x 10½

2. Referring to Quilt Layout on page 21 for Section One, sew one 10" x 10½" Fabric A piece to unit from step 1. Press. Section One is complete.

Section Two (Books)

SECTION 2	Number of Pieces	Dimensions
BOOK 1 PAGES	1	1½" x 2½"
BOOK 1 SPINE	1	1½" x 9½"
BOOK 1 COVER	1 1	1½" x 2½" 1½" square
BOOK 2 PAGES	1	1½" square
BOOK 2 SPINE	1	1½" x 7½"
BOOK 3 PAGES	1	1½" x 2½"
BOOK 3 SPINE	1	1½" x 8½"
BOOK 3 COVER	1 1	1½" x 8½" 1½" square

1. Make quick corner triangle units by sewing 1½" Fabric A square to the end of 1½" x 2½" piece (Book 1 pages). Repeat to sew 1½" square (Book 1 cover) to opposite end. Press.

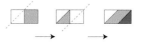

A = 1½ x 1½
Book 1 Pages = 1½ x 2½
Book 1 Cover = 1½ x 1½

17

2. Make quick corner triangle units by sewing 1½" square (Book 2 pages) to end of 1½" x 2½" piece (Book 1 cover). Press.

Book 2 Pages = 1½ x 1½
Book 1 Cover = 1½ x 2½

3. Sew unit from step 2 to top of 1½" x 7½" piece (Book 2 spine). Press.

1½

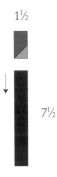

7½

4. Sew 1½" x 9½" piece (Book 1 spine) to side of unit from step 3. Press.

1½

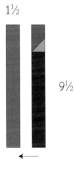

9½

5. Sew unit from step 1 to unit from step 4. Press.

6. Make quick corner triangle units by sewing one 1½" Fabric A square to the end of 1½" x 2½" piece (Book 3 pages) and one 1½" square (Book 3 cover) to opposite end. Press.

A = 1½ x 1½
Book 3 Pages = 1½ x 2½
Book 3 Cover = 1½ x 1½

7. Make quick corner triangle unit by sewing 1½" Fabric C square to end of 1½" x 8½" piece (Book 3 cover). Press.

C = 1½ x 1½
Book 3 Cover = 1½ x 8½

8. Sew 1½" x 8½" piece (Book 3 spine) to unit from step 7. Press.

1½

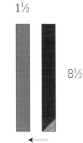

8½

9. Sew unit from step 6 between one 1½" x 2½" Fabric A piece and unit from step 8. Press.

2½

1½

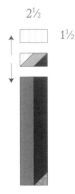

10. Sew unit from step 5 to unit from step 9. Press.

11. Add 2" x 4½" Fabric A piece to top of unit from step 10 to complete Section 2. Press.

4½

2

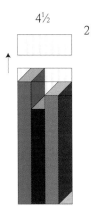

Section Two complete.

Sections Three-Five (Boxes)

SECTION 3-5		Number of Pieces	Dimensions
	BOX 1 LIGHT	1	1½" x 6½"
		1	1½" square
	BOX 1 MEDIUM	3	1½" squares
	BOX 1 DARK	1	1½" x 2½"
	BOX 2 LIGHT	1	2" x 5½"
	BOX 2 MEDIUM	1	1½" x 3"
	BOX 2 DARK	1	1½" x 5½"
		1	1½" square

Section Three

1. Make quick corner triangle unit by sewing 1½" square (Box 1 medium) to a 1½" x 2½" piece (Box 1 dark) and a 1½" Fabric C square to opposite end. Press.

Box 1 Medium = 1½ x 1½
Box 1 Dark = 1½ x 2½
C = 1½ x 1½

2. Sew a 2½" x 9½" Fabric C piece to the unit from step 1. Press

9½

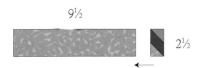

2½

3. Sew a 10 " x 10½" Fabric A piece to unit from step 2. Press.

10½

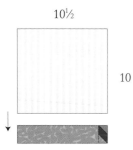

10

Section Three complete.

Section Four

1. Make quick corner triangle unit by sewing 1½" square (Box 2 dark) to one end of a 1½" x 3" piece (Box 2 medium) and a 1½" square (Box 1 medium) to opposite end. Press.

Box 2 Dark = 1½ x 1½
Box 2 Medium= 1½ x 3
Box 1 Medium = 1½ x 1½

2. Make a quick corner triangle unit by sewing a 1½" Fabric A square to the end of a 1½" x 5½" piece (Box 2 dark). Press.

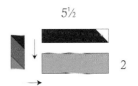

A = 1½ x 1½
Box 2 Dark = 1½ x 5½

3. Sew a 2" x 5½" piece (Box 2 light) to unit from step 2. Sew unit from step 1 to the side as shown. Press.

5½

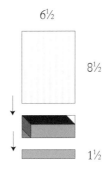

2

4. Sew unit from step 3 between a 6½" x 8½" Fabric A piece and a 1½" x 6½" piece (Box 1 light). Press.

6½

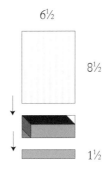

8½

1½

Section Four complete.

Section Five

1. Make a quick corner triangle unit by sewing together a 1½" square (Box 1 medium) and a 1½" Fabric C square. Sew a 1½" square (Box 1 light) to it, and press. Join this unit to a 2½" x 7½" Fabric C piece. Press.

1½   7½

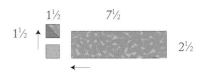

1½   2½

2. Sew unit from step 1 to 8½" x 10" Fabric A piece. Press.

8½

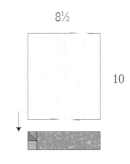

10

Section Five complete.

Section Six (Blocks)

SECTION 6	Number of Pieces	Dimensions
BLOCK 1 LIGHT *	1	3½" square
BLOCK 1 MEDIUM	1	1½" x 3½"
	1	1½" square
BLOCK 1 DARK	1	1½" square
BLOCK 2 LIGHT *	1	2½" square
BLOCK 2 MEDIUM	1	1½" x 3½"
BLOCK 2 DARK	1	1½" x 2½"
	1	1½" square

We used a fussy cut of a printed fabric to add fun motifs to the blocks.

1. Make a quick corner triangle unit by sewing 1½" square (Block 1 medium) to the end of a 1½" x 2½" piece (Block 2 dark). Press.

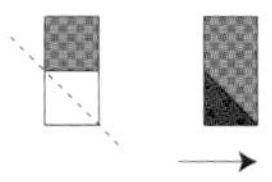

Block 1 Medium = 1½ x 1½
Block 2 Dark = 1½ x 2½

2. Sew unit from step 1 to 2½" square (Block 2 light). Press.

2½
2½

3. Make a quick corner triangle unit by sewing 1½" square (Block 2 dark) to the end of 1½" x 3½" piece (Block 2 medium) and a 1½" Fabric A square to opposite end. Press.

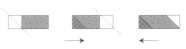

Block 2 Dark = 1½ x 1½
Block 2 Medium = 1½ x 3½
A = 1½ x 1½

4. Make a quick corner triangle unit by sewing 1½" square (Block 1 dark) to the end of 1½" x 3½" Fabric A piece. Press.

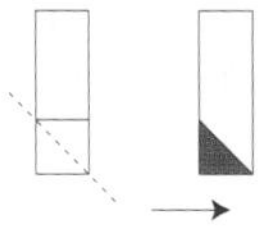

Block 1 Dark = 1½ x 1½
A = 1½ x 3½

5. Sew unit from step 3 to unit from step 2. Press. Add unit from step 4 to the side as shown. Press.

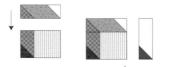

6. Make a quick corner triangle unit by sewing a 1½" Fabric C square on the end of 1½" x 3½" piece (Block 1 medium). Press.

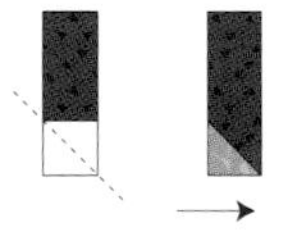

C = 1½ x 1½
Block 1 Medium = 1½ x 3½

7. Sew unit from step 6 to 3½" square (Block 1 light). Press.

3½
3½

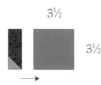

8. Sew unit from step 5 to unit from step 7. Press.

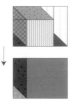

9. Make a quick corner triangle unit by sewing a 2½" Fabric C square to the end of a 2½" x 6½" Fabric A piece. Press.

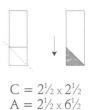

C = 2½ x 2½
A = 2½ x 6½

10. Sew unit from step 9 to unit from step 8. Press.

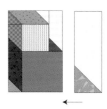

11. Sew unit from step 10 to a 6½" x 6" Fabric A piece to complete Section Six. Press.

6½

6

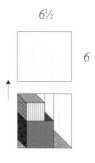

Section Six complete.

12. Sew sections 1 through 6 together. Press each seam after it's sewn.

Section 1   Section 2   Section 3   Section 4   Section 5   Section 6

Section Seven (Shelf unit)

1. Joining short ends, sew together the 1½" x 24½" and the 1½" x 20½" Fabric B pieces. Press.

2. Make two quick corner triangle units by sewing together two 1½" Fabric A squares and two 1½" Fabric D squares. Press.

A = 1½ x 1½
D = 1½ x 1½
Make 2

3. Referring to diagram for placement, sew two 1½" Fabric A squares and two 1½" Fabric B squares to units from step 2. Press.

1½   1½

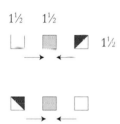   1½

Make 1 of each

4. Sew 1½" x 3½" Fabric C piece to the top of each unit from step 3. Press.

3½   3½

1½   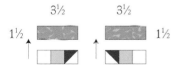   1½

5. Make quick corner triangle units by sewing remaining 1½" Fabric D squares to two corners of 2½" x 36½" Fabric A strip.

D = 1½ x 1½
A = 2½ x 36½

6. Sew unit from step 5 between two units from step 4 and two 1½" x 2½" Fabric A pieces. Press.

1½   1½

2½

7. Referring to diagram, sew together strip from step 1 and unit from step 6. Press each seam after it is sewn. Join to unit from step 12 of Section 6 to complete background. Press.

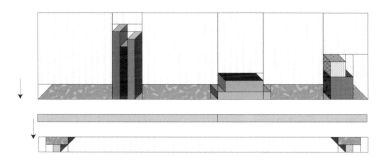

Adding the Borders

1. Cut one 1¼" x 42" accent border strip in half crosswise and sew half to an end of each of two accent border strips.

2. Repeat step 1 to join outside border strips.

3. Sew accent border strips and outside border strips together lengthwise in pairs of the same length. Referring to Mitered Borders directions on page 110, add mitered borders to the quilt.

Adding the Appliqués

Refer to Quick-Fuse Appliqué directions on page 109. Trace appliqué designs from pages 10, 12, 13, and 15 and quick-fuse to wall quilt, referring to the color photo on page 21 and layout on page 16 for placement.

Layering and Finishing

1. Arrange and baste backing, batting, and top together, referring to Layering the Quilt directions on page 110.

2. Machine or hand quilt as desired.

3. Cut one 2¾" x 42" binding piece in half and sew each to the ends of a binding piece. Refer to Binding the Quilt on page 111 and add binding to your quilt.

Elf Tip

Don't have a mobile apparatus? String your toy shapes together with ribbon to make a garland to hang from a shelf, window, or another place where baby can see the whimsical toys. When baby outgrows the mobile or garland, use the toy shapes as ornaments on your Christmas tree.

TOYS MADE HERE

Twirling Toys Baby Mobile

Materials Needed:

Five scraps approximately 8" x 12" in various colors for background shapes
Various scraps for appliqués
½ yard each of five coordinating ribbons
½ yard heavyweight fusible web
Batting or polyester fiber clusters for stuffing
Mobile apparatus (we found ours at a second-hand shop)
Optional: Approximately ¼ yard of two fabrics for decorative sleeves (depends on mobile)

1. Using a copy machine, reduce appliqué patterns on pages 10, 12, 14, and 15 by 50%.

2. Draw appliqué patterns of your choice onto paper side of fusible web. Refer to Quick-Fuse Appliqué on page 109 to prepare appliqué shapes.

3. Cut background fabrics into shapes to complement appliqués selected. We used a circle for the lamb, square for the horse, rectangle for the train, and an oval for the teddy bear. We chose a star for the middle of our mobile. Be sure background shape is large enough for the appliqué and include ¼" seam allowance on all sides. Cut a front and a back.

4. With right sides together, sew shapes together leaving an opening for turning and stuffing.

5. Turn each shape right side out. Press. Center prepared appliqué pieces on each shape and fuse following the manufacturer's recommendations.

6. Use embroidery floss to add eyes and other details.

7. Stuff each shape and hand stitch the opening closed.

8. Attach ribbons to hang shapes from the mobile, adding a bow for decoration. Make sure your mobile is well balanced.
Optional: To add more color, we made sleeves for our mobile apparatus. Cut fabric double the length of your mobile pieces so that the fabric can be softly gathered after it's sewn. Dimensions will depend on your mobile.

Elwood & Ella Santa's Elves

Elwood & Ella ~ Santa's Elves

Finished size: 17" tall

Elwood and Ella will captivate your family as they peek through the tree boughs or hold gifts in their arms. Lanky legs, pointed ears, and boots with turned-up toes adorned with jingle bells accent these three-dimensional characters.

Materials Needed

For each elf:

Body - ³⁄₈ yard
Legs - ¹⁄₈ yard
Shirt - ¹⁄₄ yard
Overalls (boy) - ¹⁄₃ yard
Jumper (girl) - ¹⁄₄ yard
Hat - ¹⁄₄ yard of Berber fleece
Collar, Cuff - ¹⁄₆ yard of
 Berber fleece
Lining - Scraps
Boots - 5" x 10" piece of felt
Polyester Stuffing
Tiny bells for collar, boots,
 and hat
Jute or yarn for hair

24

Making the Bodies

1. Trace body pieces on pages 27-29 onto paper for a pattern, matching dots to join pieces and including all markings. Position leg and body patterns onto the wrong side of a double thickness of fabric and trace around each piece. Stitch on drawn lines leaving openings for ears and stuffing. Trim ¼" from stitched lines, clipping at neck, thumbs, under the arms, and curve on foot. Turn and press.

2. Turn under ½" seam allowance on lower edge of body and press.

3. Firmly stuff lower arms. Stitch along marked area to define arm joints. Continue stuffing arms and stitch at shoulders.

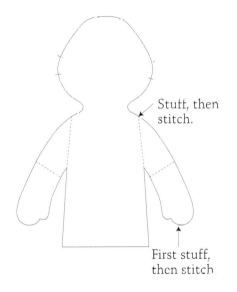

Stuff, then stitch.

First stuff, then stitch.

4. Stuff head and neck firmly, then upper body loosely. To make your elf sturdier, insert a craft stick or a 4" - 5" piece of ¼" dowel into the head, neck, and upper body.

5. To add weight to the body, make a pouch to fill with sand or plastic pellets. Begin with a 4½" x 5½" piece of fabric. Fold it in half crosswise and stitch, leaving a 2" opening. Fill and stitch across the top. Position in the lower body with stuffing.

6. Stuff legs and pin to lower body with seams at the top and back of leg and the feet pointing upward. Stitch across lower body catching legs in the seam.

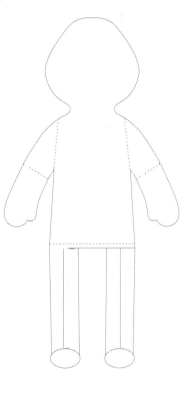

7. Trace around elf ears on wrong side of fabric. Layer two earpieces, right sides together, with lightweight batting on bottom and stitch on drawn line, leaving one edge open as shown on pattern piece. Cut ¼" from stitched line and turn right side out. Press. Stitch ear design through all three layers by hand or machine. Insert an ear at each opening on sides of face and slipstitch in place.

8. Trace nose pattern onto fabric and cut out. Fold right sides together, stitch seam, turn, and lightly stuff. Use a needle and double thread to baste and gather a circle ⅛" from the raw edge of nose. Tie off gathering stitches and stitch nose to marked position on face.

Fold

Gathering line

9. Draw facial features on the elf face with a fine line permanent ink pen or paint. Use blush or colored pencil to add color to the cheeks.

Clothes for Elwood

Make patterns on pages 28, 30-31 and pin on fabric. Follow the markings and instructions given on each pattern piece and use ¼" seams.

Shirt

1. Turn center back seam under ¼" and stitch. Sew shirt back to front at shoulders, sleeves, and sides. Clip under arms, turn right side out, and press.

2. For collar and cuffs, iron lightweight fusible web to the back of a 6" x 8" piece of lining, following manufacturer's instructions. Fuse lining to a 6" x 8" square of Berber fleece. Pin collar pattern to fused Berber and cut out. Stitch neck to shirt, easing to fit. Sew tiny bells to tips of shirt collar.

3. Cut two 1½" x 6½" pieces of Berber fleece for cuffs. With right sides together, stitch cuff along short edge. Turn and pin right side of cuff to inside of shirt sleeve. Stitch and turn cuff to outside of shirt. Place on elf and tack in the back to close.

Overalls

1. Cut out overall pattern. Stitch together at side and leg seams. Clip and press.

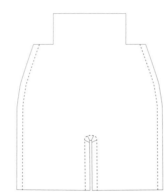

2. Stitch facing pieces together between dots at sides.

3. Cut two 1½" x 5" pieces of overall fabric for straps. Fold in half lengthwise with right sides together. Stitch along side and one end. Clip corners and turn. Press.

4. Position straps at the top of overall front approximately ½" from sides of bib and pin. With right sides together, pin facing in place on the outside of overalls. Stitch along top edge of overalls. Clip corners. Turn facing to the inside and press.

5. Turn under ¼" on leg bottoms. Hand stitch a running stitch with double thread or perle cotton and gather to fit elf legs. Place overalls on elf, adjust straps, and tack in place. Tie off thread at legs to secure.

Hat and Hair

1. Cut out hat and 10" x 1½" contrasting band. Stitch hat seams and turn right side out.

2. Stitch band together at short ends. Pin right side of band to wrong side of hat, easing to fit, and stitch in place. Turn band to outside and sew a ½" bell on the hat tip. We added a little stuffing to the end of Elwood's hat for body. (For Ella's hat, we tacked the hat tip to the brim.)

3. For hair, cut three 6" pieces of jute or yarn. Fold in half and stitch together at fold. Stitch by hand to center top seam of head. Untwist jute to frazzle his hair. Place hat on his head.

Boots

With wrong sides together, place boot pieces together in pairs. With a ⅛" seam, stitch around sides and bottom of boots. Add bells or beads for decorations and place on Elwood's feet.

Clothes for Ella

Shirt

Refer to the instructions for Elwood's shirt and repeat shirt instructions 1-3. If desired, make Ella's collar with the rounded shape and add a button at the center front. Instead of cuffs, we rolled up Ella's sleeves. Place on Ella and tack to close.

Jumper

1. Using the same pattern as overalls, cut jumper top and facing as directed on pattern. Sew the pairs together at side seams using a ⅜" seam. Turn right side out.

2. For skirt, cut a 20" x 5¾" fabric piece and stitch together at short ends. Press. Gather one long edge with a basting thread.

3. With right sides together, pin skirt gathers to jumper top. Adjust gathers and stitch.

4. To attach straps and facing, repeat steps 3 and 4 of Overalls on page 26. Slipstitch facing to skirt if desired. Hem skirt by double turning ¼" and stitching along bottom edge. Add ⅛" rickrack ¼" from bottom edge of skirt if desired. Place on Ella, adjust straps, and tack in the back to secure. We add two ⅝" buttons on the jumper front.

Bloomers (Optional)

1. Trace bottom section of overalls for pattern. Stitch side and inside leg seams. Double turn bottom edges and stitch. Turn waist under ¼" and gather with a double basting thread. Put bloomers on Ella, position gathers, and tie off ends.

Boots

Make the same as for Elwood.

Hair

For hair, wrap yarn 40 to 50 times around a 2" x 5" piece of cardboard. Stitch yarn together at fold on one side of cardboard. Cut yarn on other side of cardboard. Make four or five sets. Stitch to back and top of head using a backstitch.

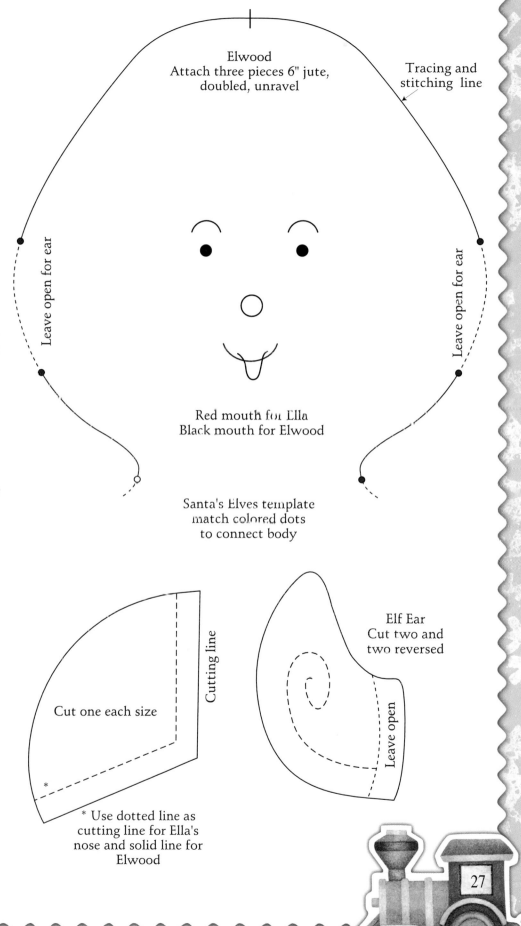

Elwood
Attach three pieces 6" jute, doubled, unravel

Tracing and stitching line

Leave open for ear

Leave open for ear

Red mouth for Ella
Black mouth for Elwood

Santa's Elves template match colored dots to connect body

Stitching line

Cut loops

Cutting line

Cut one each size

*

Elf Ear
Cut two and two reversed

Leave open

* Use dotted line as cutting line for Ella's nose and solid line for Elwood

27

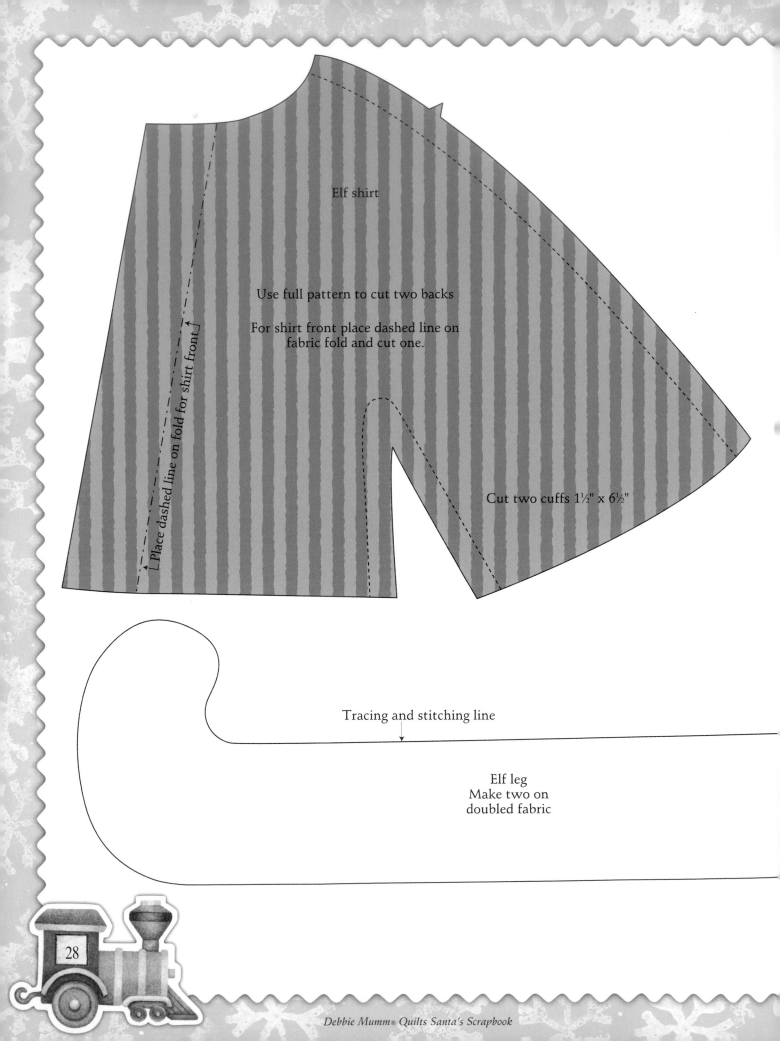

Elf shirt

Use full pattern to cut two backs

For shirt front place dashed line on
fabric fold and cut one.

Place dashed line on fold for shirt front

Cut two cuffs 1½" x 6½"

Tracing and stitching line

Elf leg
Make two on
doubled fabric

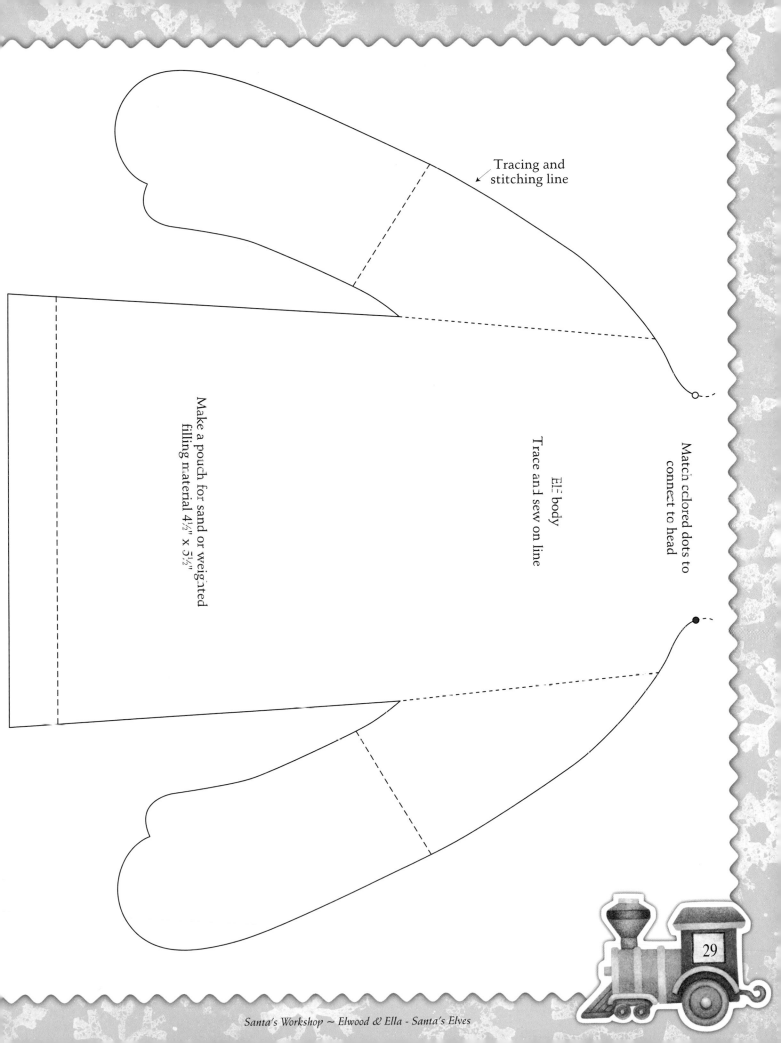

Tracing and
stitching line

Match colored dots to
connect to head

Make a pouch for sand or weighted
filling material 4½" x 5½"

Elf body
Trace and sew on line

29

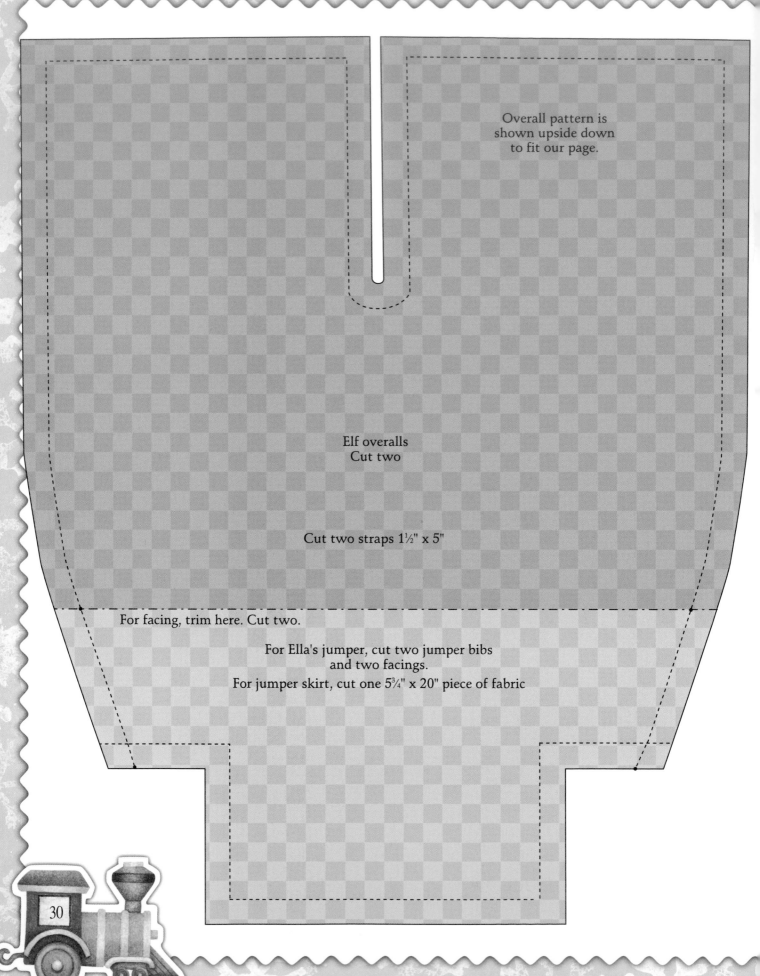

Overall pattern is
shown upside down
to fit our page.

Elf overalls
Cut two

Cut two straps 1½" x 5"

For facing, trim here. Cut two.

For Ella's jumper, cut two jumper bibs
and two facings.
For jumper skirt, cut one 5¾" x 20" piece of fabric

30

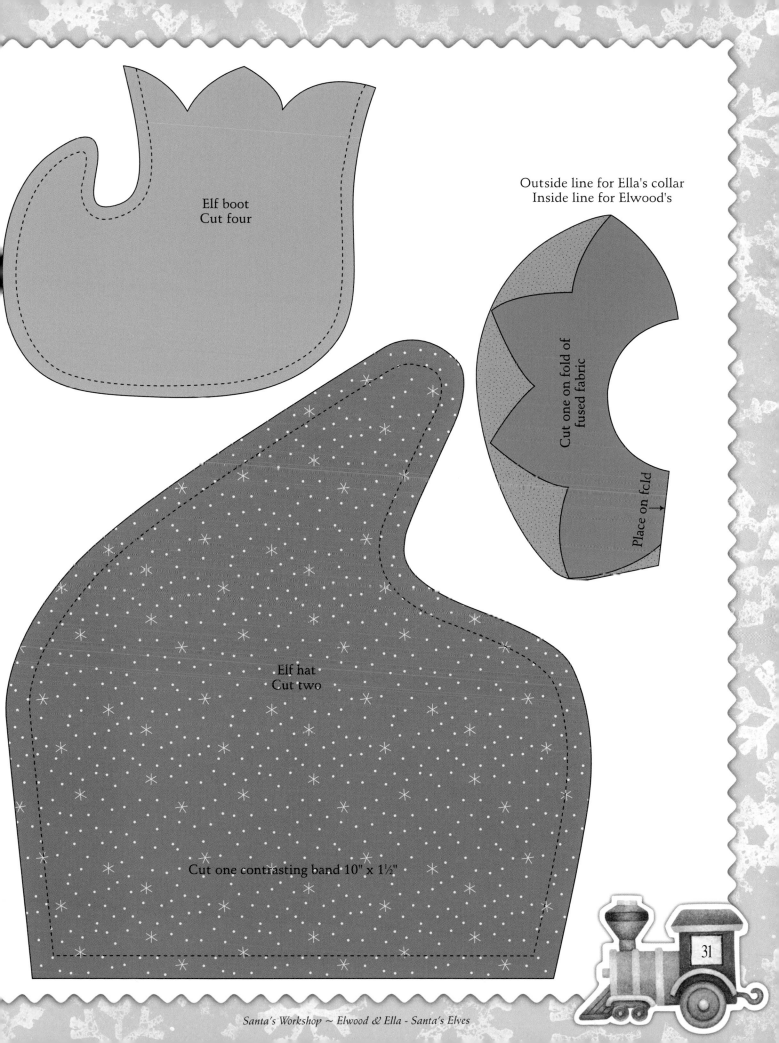

Elf boot
Cut four

Outside line for Ella's collar
Inside line for Elwood's

Cut one on fold of fused fabric

Place on fold

Elf hat
Cut two

Cut one contrasting band 10" x 1½"

31

Everything Elfish Miniature Christmas Tree

Everything Elfish Miniature Christmas Tree

*This teensy tree decorated with tiny flannel elf boots,
bells, and bows will jingle its way into your heart.
A miniature tree skirt uses easy sewing
techniques for a charming effect.*

Materials Needed

Small Christmas Tree - about
    18"-24" in height, live
    or artificial
Red tree skirt fabric - ⅜ yard
Green tree skirt fabric - ⅜ yard
Assorted scraps and pieces
    for stockings
Bells - Twelve 1" for tree;
    thirty-five ⅜" for star;
    eight ⁵⁄₁₆" for tree skirt
Ribbon - ⅛" wide, 2 yards
Tin star - 4" wide, or
    appropriate size for
    your tree
Metallic floss to hang
    stockings
Template Plastic
Hot glue gun and glue sticks
Gum drops, gummy bears,
    small candy canes,
    and other treats to
    fill the stockings
Garland of gold beads

Making the Stockings

1. Cut two 4½" squares from each of your assorted festive fabrics. Cut as many as you will need to adorn your miniature tree; we made fourteen.

2. Trace elf stocking pattern on page 34 onto template plastic and cut out.

3. With wrong sides together, position fabric squares together and trace around template on right side of fabric.

4. Leaving top of stocking open, sew on drawn line. Trim seam allowance to ⅛" and trim stocking top along drawn line.

5. Trace elf stocking cuff pattern on page 34 onto template plastic or paper and cut out. Position on fabric for cuff, trace, and cut out. Glue or fuse onto stocking top. Stitch back seam of cuff using the same seam line as stocking.

6. Cut 5" pieces of metallic floss to make loops for hanging. Hand stitch through the top of the back seam and tie. Fill your elf stockings with candy or other treats and they're ready to hang on the tree.

Making the Tree Skirt

1. From both the red and green tree skirt fabrics, cut two 12" squares and two 1" x 4¾" pieces. Set small pieces aside.

2. Trace tree skirt pattern on page 34 onto paper or template plastic, transferring cut marks and placement directions.

3. Fold one red and one green 12" fabric square in half and then in half again. Fold square diagonally so that one side is triple folded and another double folded.

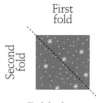

First fold

Second fold

Folded twice

4. Place skirt template on folded fabric, matching folded sides with markings on template. Cut where indicated. Repeat for both red and green folded pieces.

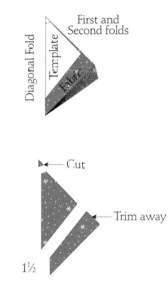

First and Second folds

Diagonal Fold

Template

Fabric

Cut

Trim away

1½

5. With right sides together, place cut tree skirt tops from step 4 onto remaining 12" red and green squares. Using a ¼" seam, stitch around cut edges and circle. Trim and clip seams. Referring to diagram, cut from one short side to center hole. Turn right side out and press.

Cut here

6. Sew 1" x 4¾" pieces of red and green fabric to right sides of cut edges of corresponding tree skirts, matching colors. Press seam toward binding.

7. Press under ¼" on remaining edges. Fold binding over to stitching line and hand or machine stitch in place.

8. Overlap red and green skirts, so all points are exposed. Stitch around circle from point A (opening at red skirt) to point B (opening at green skirt).

Bound opening on bottom skirt

B A

Bound opening on top skirt

9. Sew bells at the points on both skirt layers.

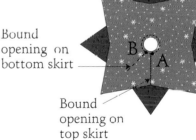

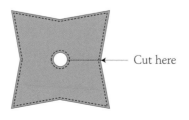

Adding the Finishing Touches

1. Cut ⅛" wide ribbon into 6" lengths and use to tie 1" bells to tree.

2. Glue small bells to the edges of tin star using hot glue gun and glue sticks.

3. Decorate the tree with a miniature garland. Hang your stockings and bells on the tree, encircle the bottom with the tree skirt, and place the star on the treetop.

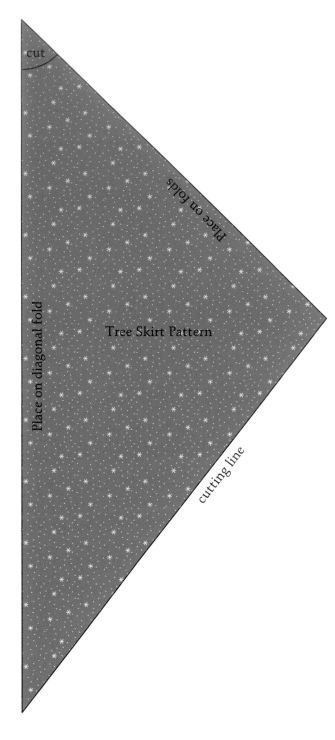

Tree Skirt Pattern

cut

place on folds

Place on diagonal fold

cutting line

Elf Stocking Pattern

1.
Trace on doubled fabric.
2.
Stitch on drawn line then cut ⅞" from seam.

Elf Stocking Cuff Pattern

Easy Ornaments Children Can Make

Cinnamon Ornaments

Mix 1 cup ground cinnamon and ¾ cup applesauce to form a stiff dough. Roll out to ¼" thickness. Let the children cut the dough with cookie cutters. Using a small straw or large toothpick, make a small hole in each ornament for ribbon hangers. Let air dry about one week, turning over occasionally; or bake at 200 degrees for 1½ hours. After drying, the kids can decorate with Royal icing (see below) or dimensional paints.

Wreath-framed Photo

Cut a circular shape from cardboard. Glue child's photo in the center. Using the holly pattern on page 63, cut holly leaves from two shades of green felt. Glue holly leaves around photo on cardboard. Add red buttons or beads for holly berries. Cover back with a piece of felt or more holly leaves. Punch a hole and add a ribbon or piece of metallic embroidery floss for a hanger.

Terrific Toys

The appliqué patterns for the Toyland Quilt on pages 10-15 are easily adapted to become ornaments. You may want to reduce the patterns by 50% on a copier before starting if smaller ornaments are desired. Trace basic designs (such as entire train engine) on an appropriate color of felt. Cut two of each basic shape. Glue the two pieces together so that your ornaments are two-sided and have enough body to hang on the tree. Let the kids add details to the basic shapes using rickrack, buttons, felt pieces, and other embellishments from your sewing box. Thread a piece of embroidery floss or ribbon through each ornament to serve as a hanger.

Easy "Gingerbread" House

Use an empty and rinsed ½ pint cardboard milk or juice container as the base for your gingerbread house. Break graham crackers to the size of the sides of milk container and using Royal Icing, adhere graham crackers, covering the milk carton. Using the icing, adhere cereal, pretzels, hard candies, red hots, and other kitchen "finds" to add details to your gingerbread house. Add a ribbon to use as a hanger, or set your house on a shelf or window sill.

Royal Icing

Use this icing to decorate your Cinnamon Ornaments or Easy "Gingerbread" House. When dry, it firms and hardens.
1¼ cups sifted confectioners' sugar
1 egg white
1 teaspoon strained lemon juice
Beat ¾ cup of the sugar with egg white and lemon juice until thick and white (about 10 minutes). Add the remaining ½ cup sugar and beat until stiff. Icing may be tinted with food coloring.

35

Turned-up Toes Christmas Stockings

Turned-up Toes Christmas Stockings

*Imagine the looks of wonder in their eyes when your
family sees these whimsical stockings on Christmas morning!
Anything goes on these stockings!
We used felt and velvet, buttons and brocade,
trims, ribbons, and bells. Have fun!*

Materials Needed
Makes two stockings
Stocking - ½ yard felted wool,
    felt, or velvet
Stocking cuffs - ¼ yard velvet
    or brocade
Lining (may use cuff fabric
    above or cotton)- ¼ yard
Decorative trims, cording,
    and threads
Polyester stuffing

Elf Tip
*It's simple to give your wool
an added richness and
fullness ... felt it!
An easy way to do this is to
simmer your wool fabric in
boiling water for 20 minutes,
then plunge it into icy water.
After this process, put it in
the dryer until thoroughly
dry. The result is a thicker,
fuller fabric that will give
added texture to your
stockings. Don't forget to
use added yardage to
account for shrinkage!*

Making the Stockings

1. Trace the stocking top, middle, and toe sections onto paper. Cut out and join sections at dots to make stocking pattern.

2. With wrong sides together, pin stocking pattern onto folded fabric and cut out.

3. Stitch decorative trims to stocking front. A general placement line is marked on the pattern. For variety, we sewed our first trim above the line on one stocking, below the line on another stocking, and right on the line for the third stocking.

4. With wrong sides together, stitch around stocking with a scant ¼" seam allowance, leaving stocking top open.

5. Blanket stitch with decorative thread over machine stitching.

6. Trace stocking cuff onto paper to make pattern.

7. Cut ¼ yard of cuff fabric in half crosswise, making two 21" x 9" pieces. Fold each in half crosswise. Place cuff pattern on one piece of folded fabric and pin. Be sure to place marked pattern edge onto fabric fold. Cut around pattern edge. Repeat to make lining.

8. With cuff and lining positioned right sides together, begin stitching at marked box and stitch along pointed edge, pivoting at dots and ending stitching line at other marked box. Clip tips and angles, turn right side out, and press (only finger press if using velvet). Fold cuff right sides together and stitch side seams together.

9. With right side of cuff and wrong side of stocking together, position cuff inside stocking matching raw edges.

10. Insert a 6" loop of decorative cord between stocking and cuff at back edge for hanging.

11. Stitch around top of stocking using a ½" seam. Fold cuff and cording to outside of stocking.

12. Add a small amount of polyester stuffing to toe of stocking to give it shape. Add more decorative trims to stocking if desired.

Place on fold

Stocking Cuff
Cut two on fold (one cuff, one lining)

Loop placement

Begin stitching

Stocking Middle

Turned-up Toes Christmas Stocking Top

Stocking and cuff seam line

Stocking Toe

Placement line for trims

Trace stocking pieces, joining segments at matching dots

39

Off to Work Tool Carrier

Off To Work Tool Carrier

Materials Needed

Homemade or purchased
  wooden toolbox
Acrylic craft paints: light
  ivory, ivory, tan, medium
  brown, medium gray,
  antique gold, charcoal,
  medium red, dark green
Assorted paintbrushes
Crackle medium
Sea sponge
Snowflake stencil or stamp
Scotch Magic™ Tape
Ruler, pencil, ballpoint pen
Tracing paper
Graphite transfer paper
Extra fine black permanent
  ink pen
Matte spray varnish

*You'll be inspired to "tool-up" for other projects with this
charming, painted tool caddy. We give directions on how to
paint this indispensable carryall. Add your own name to
replace Santa's or just use "toolbox" if your carrier
is a smaller size. Read all instructions before beginning.*

Painting the Toolbox

Refer to the color photo for guidance as needed.

1. Base coat sides of toolbox with ivory paint, outside end sections with dark green, and inside with medium red. Several coats may be required for good coverage.

2. Base coat handle with medium brown. Dry thoroughly.

3. Following manufacturer's directions, apply crackle medium to painted handle. Allow to "set" according to manufacturer's specifications.

4. Apply a quick, even coat of antique gold paint to handle. Crackles will appear in painted surface. Do not touch, as surface is very fragile when wet. Dry thoroughly.

5. With ruler, measure one inch up from bottom on sides and make a few small marks with a pencil to serve as a guideline. Apply strip of Scotch Magic™ Tape along bottom of guideline on both sides of box.

Sponge and stencil above tape

Tape 1"

6. Using sea sponge, sponge tan paint over ivory basecoat above tape on both sides of box. Apply lightly for a mottled effect. Dry thoroughly.

7. Using a purchased stencil or stamp and following manufacturer's directions, add light ivory snowflakes randomly on the sponged sides. Dry thoroughly. Remove tape.

8. Place strip of Scotch Magic™ Tape above your 1" guideline. Use the ruler and a pencil to mark checks every ½" in area below tape. Place strip of tape along bottom edge of box ½" below other tape. Paint every other square medium red in the area left exposed. Dry thoroughly. Remove bottom tape.

Tape
½"
½"
Tape

9. Place strip of Scotch Magic™ Tape over painted checks. Paint bottom row of checks using a checkerboard pattern. Allow to dry thoroughly then remove tape.

10. Mark and paint charcoal and ivory checks on angled portion of the end pieces and on top edge of side pieces.

11. Enlarge "Santa's Toolbox" pattern on a copier to a size that fits your toolbox. Trace enlarged pattern onto tracing paper. Position tracing paper on toolbox where desired. Tape in place leaving one side open. Slide graphite paper under tracing paper and using ballpoint pen, transfer design. Remove tape, tracing, and graphite paper.

12. Using charcoal, medium gray, antique gold, and medium red paint, paint design as indicated in photo. Allow to dry thoroughly.

13. Using fine point permanent ink pen, add details to the painted elements and measuring marks to the capital "S".

14. Apply several coats of matte spray varnish, following manufacturer's directions.

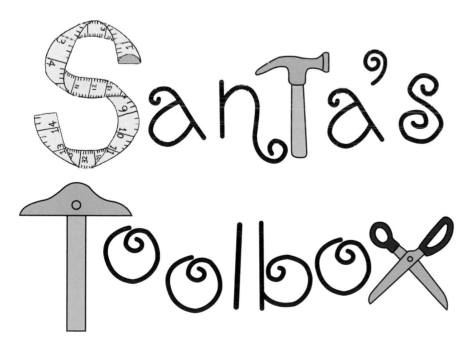

41

#1 North Pole Lane

DEAR SANTA,

My name is Bobby and I have ... this year. I would really like t... firetruck. The kind that has ... and has a dalmatian dog. I re... Maybe you could bring me a ... or the red wagon you gav...

Mrs. Claus in her apron
has projects to make,
The table to set, and
gingerbread to bake.
Her teapot collection
is all in a row,
While on her crazy quilt
she continues to sew.

Christmas Tea Wall Quilt

Christmas Tea Wall Quilt
Finished size: 32" x 31½"
Photo Page 47

Mrs. Claus' collection of charming Christmas teapots is displayed on this delightful wall quilt made to resemble a quaint cupboard. Machine appliquéd teapots feature button embellishments. The cupboard is easily pieced and your quilting technique can accent the architectural elements. Read all instructions before beginning and use ¼"-wide seams throughout.

Fabric Requirements

Shelf Background - ⅝ yard
Shelves and Outside Border
   ½ yard
Middle Border - ½ yard
Corner Squares - ⅛ yard
Accent Border - ⅛ yard
Arch trim - ⅛ yard
Teapots - Assorted scraps
   and pieces
Backing - 1 yard
Thermal fleece batting
   36" x 36" piece
Buttons for embellishment
Lightweight fusible web
   1 yard
Stabilizer - 1 yard

44

Cutting the Strips and Pieces

Before you begin, read Cutting the Strips and Pieces on page 108.

		FIRST CUT		SECOND CUT	
		Number of Strips or Pieces	Dimensions	Number of Strips or Pieces	Dimensions
	SHELF BACK-GROUND	2	7½" x 42"	2	7½" x 20½"
				1	7½" x 3½"
		1	5" x 42"	1	5" x 20½"
	SHELVES & OUTSIDE BORDER	3	1½" x 42"	3	1½" x 20½"
		4	2" x 42"	2	2" x 30½"
				1	2" x 33½"
				1	2" x 26½"
	MIDDLE BORDER	1	4" x 42"	1	4" x 21½"
		3	3" x 42"	2	3" x 24"
				1	3" x 21½"
	CORNER SQUARES	4	3" squares		
	ACCENT BORDER	2	1" x 42"	2	1" x 22"
	ARCH TRIM	1	1½" x 42"	1	1½" x 21½"

Assembling the Cupboard

1. Sew together the three 1½" x 20½" shelf pieces and one 5" x 20½" and two 7½" x 20½" shelf background pieces in the order shown. Press.

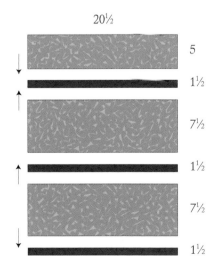

20½

5

1½

7½

1½

7½

1½

2. Sew 1" x 22" accent borders to the sides of unit from step 1. Press. Sew 3" x 21½" middle border piece to the bottom of unit. Press.

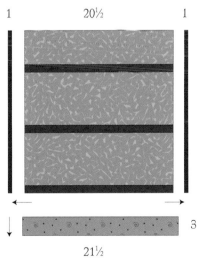

1   20½   1

22

21½   3

3. Sew together lengthwise a 4" x 21½" middle border piece and a 1½" x 21½" arch trim piece. Press.

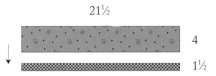

21½

4

1½

4. Using arch pattern on page 48 to make template, trace onto 7½" x 3½" shelf background piece and cut out arch adding ¼" seam allowance if hand appliquéing. Center arch at bottom of unit and appliqué to unit from step 3, referring to appliqué directions on page 109.

5. Sew unit from step 4 to unit from step 2. Press.

6. Sew 3" x 24" middle border strip between two 3" corner squares. Repeat to make 2. Press.

Make 2

7. Sew units from step 6 to the sides of cupboard unit from step 5. Press.

8. Sew a 2" x 26½" outside border strip to the bottom of unit from step 7.

9. Sew two 2" x 30½" outside border strips to the sides of cupboard unit. Press.

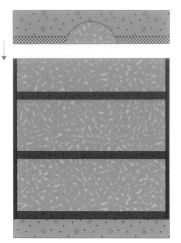

Elf Tip

Add a Little Trapunto
As an optional finishing touch for your china cupboard, how about adding strips of trapunto quilting on the outside borders? We stitched several sets of parallel lines, about ⅜" apart, on each outside border strip. Using a trapunto needle, we then pulled soft, thick yarn through the quilt front and inserted it between the stitched lines. It created just the right furniture-trim effect.

46

Assembly

1. Referring to Quick-Fuse Appliqué Instructions on page 109, trace teapot appliqué patterns from pages 48-54 and fuse to quilt. Use color photo for placement.

2. To add the top outside border, center and stitch a 2" x 33½" outside border strip to the top of finished unit from step 9. Strip will extend 2" beyond cupboard on each side. Press seam toward shelves.

3. On wrong side of this added strip, make a pencil mark ¼" from outside top edge corners. Draw diagonal line from this point to end of seam line on strip. This will be the stitching line.

4. Layer batting, backing (right side up), and quilt top (right side down) together. Using ¼" seam allowance stitch around outside edge, leaving an 8" opening at the bottom for turning. At top cupboard trim strip, pivot at corners and stitch along drawn line. Trim ¼" from diagonal stitch line.

5. Turn quilt right side out and press edges. Hand stitch opening closed.

6. Quilt as desired and embellish with buttons. We used Debbie Mumm® ceramic buttons from Mill Hill on the teapots and plain red buttons for the holly.

33½

2

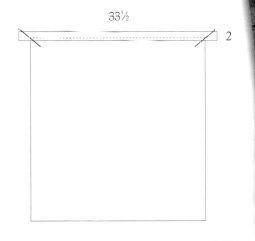

Elf Tip

Debbie Mumm® ceramic buttons can be ordered online at www.millhill.com or by calling (800) 356-9438. We used Christmas Tea Set #43161 and Crossed Candy Canes #43164 for this wall quilt.

Tracing Line _____

Tracing Line _ _ _ _ _ _ _ _ _ _ _ _
(will be hidden behind other fabrics)

Appliqué patterns are reversed for use with quick-fuse technique.

Holly template

Template for arch
Add ¼" seam allowance for hand appliqué

48

Tracing Line _____

Tracing Line _ _ _ _ _ _ _ _ _ _
(will be hidden behind other fabrics)

Appliqué shape _ . _ . _ . _ . _
placement line

*Appliqué pattern is reversed for
use with quick-fuse technique.*

Tracing Line _____

Tracing Line - - - - - - - - - - -
(will be hidden behind other fabrics)

Appliqué shape - - - - - - - -
placement line

Appliqué pattern is reversed for use with quick-fuse technique.

50

51

Tracing Line _____

Tracing Line _ _ _ _ _ _ _ _ _ _ _ _
(will be hidden behind other fabrics)

*Appliqué pattern is reversed for
use with quick-fuse technique.*

52

Tracing Line _____

Tracing Line - - - - - - - - - - - - -
(will be hidden behind other fabrics)

*Appliqué patterns are reversed for
use with quick-fuse technique.*

53

Tracing Line _____

Tracing Line _ _ _ _ _ _ _ _ _ _ _ _
(will be hidden behind other fabrics)

*Appliqué pattern is reversed for
use with quick-fuse technique.*

54

Gingerbread Cookies

½ cup butter or margarine, softened
½ cup firmly packed brown sugar
½ cup molasses
1 egg
3½ cups all-purpose flour
1 tsp baking powder
½ tsp baking soda
½ tsp salt
1 tsp ground cinnamon
½ tsp ground ginger
¼ tsp ground nutmeg
¼ tsp ground cloves
½ cup buttermilk

1. Using mixer or spoon, cream butter. Gradually add sugar, beating until light and fluffy. Add molasses and egg, mixing well.

2. Combine flour, baking powder, soda, salt, and spices, mixing well. Add to creamed mixture alternating with buttermilk, beginning and ending with flour mixture. Shape into a ball; cover and chill 2 hours.

3. Roll dough to ¼ inch thickness on a lightly floured surface. Cut into desired shapes. Place 2 inches apart on lightly greased baking sheets.

4. Bake at 375° for 10 minutes. Remove to wire racks to cool. Decorate with your favorite frosting and small candies. Store in airtight containers. Makes about 3 dozen cookies.

Elf Tip

Cute gift container for your cookies!
Measure and cut a piece of festive fabric to fit around an empty coffee can or similar container with a tight fitting lid. Using the gingerbread kids templates on page 69, cut and quick-fuse felt gingerbread kids to the fabric. Decorate the gingerbread kids by gluing on rickrack, beads, buttons, and other embellishments. Glue fabric onto the container. Use a piece of rickrack, ribbon, or cord to hide raw edges at top and bottom of container. Glue pieces of candy to the lid and you have a charming way to present your gift.

55

Christmas Ribbon Table Quilt

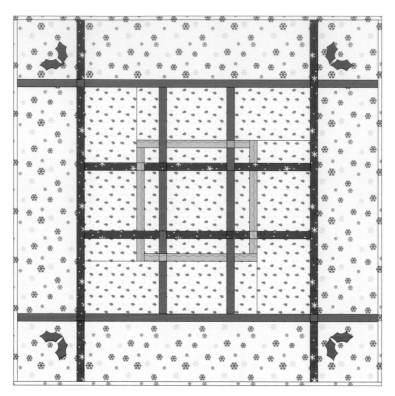

Christmas Ribbon Table Quilt
Finished size: 49" square
Photo Page 59

Fabric Requirements

Gold - ⅛ yard
Red - ¼ yard
Green - ¼ yard
Background - ⅞ yard
Outside Border - 1 yard
Binding - ½ yard
Backing - 3⅛ yards
Batting- 53" square piece
Optional: lightweight fusible
    web - ⅛ yard

Fabric ribbons of red, green, and gold intertwine on this easy table quilt. A holiday print adds charm to the border and holly appliqués accent each corner. Read all instructions before beginning and use ¼"-wide seams throughout.

Cutting the Strips and Pieces

Before you begin, read Cutting the Strips and Pieces on page 108.

	FIRST CUT		SECOND CUT	
	Number of Strips or Pieces	Dimensions	Number of Pieces	Dimensions
GOLD RIBBON	2	1½" x 42"	4	1½" x 8½"
			4	1½" x 3½"
			4	1½" x 2½"
			4	1½" squares
RED RIBBON	5	1½" x 42"	2	1½" x 39½"
			2	1½" x 10½"
			4	1½" x 8½"
			2	1½" x 7½"
			2	1½" x 3½"
GREEN RIBBON	5	1½" x 42"	2	1½" x 30½"
			2	1½" x 10½"
			6	1½" x 8½"
			2	1½" x 7½"
			2	1½" x 3½"
			2	1½" squares
BACK-GROUND	1	10½" x 42"	4	10½" x 7½"
	1	8½" x 42"	1	8½" square
			4	8½" x 7½"
	2	2½" x 42"	4	2½" x 8½"
			4	2½" squares
	1	3½" x 42"	4	3½" x 7½"
BORDERS				
OUTSIDE BORDER	4	8½" x 42"	4	8½" x 30½"
			4	8½" squares
BINDING	5	2¾" x 42"		

Making the Center

1. Sew a 1½" x 8½" gold ribbon piece between a 2½" x 8½" and a 8½" x 7½" background piece. Press. Make four.

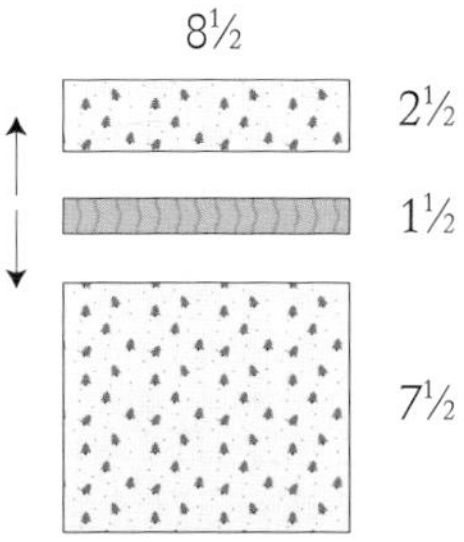

Make 4

2. Sew a 1½" x 8½" red ribbon piece to the top of two units from step 1. Press. Make two.

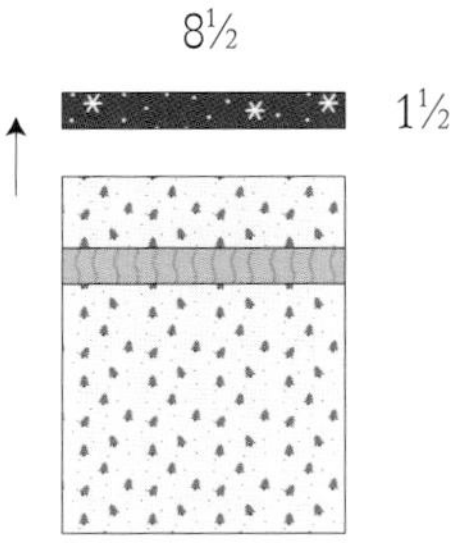

Make 2

3. Sew an 8½" background square between two 1½" x 8½" green ribbon pieces. Press.

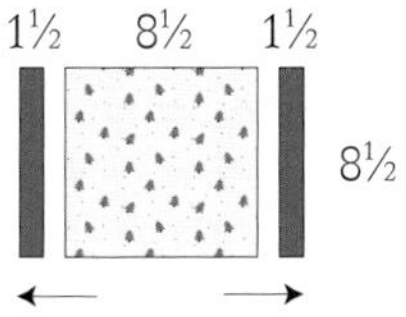

4. Sew unit from step 3 between two remaining units from step 1. Press.

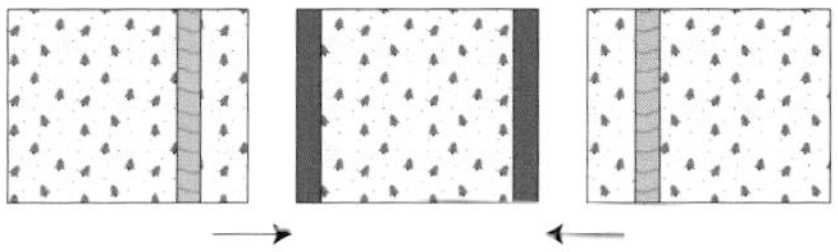

5. Sew a 2½" background square to a 1½" x 2½" gold ribbon piece. Press. Make four.

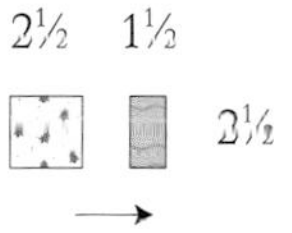

Make 4

6. Sew a 1½" x 3½" gold ribbon piece between a 3½" x 7½" background piece and unit from step 5. Press. Make four.

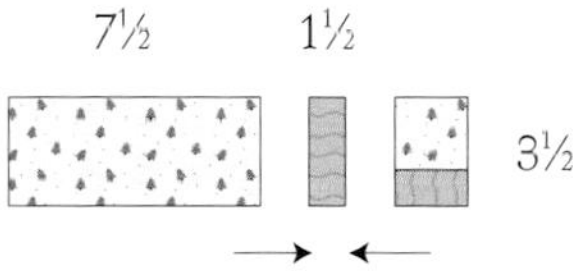

Make 4

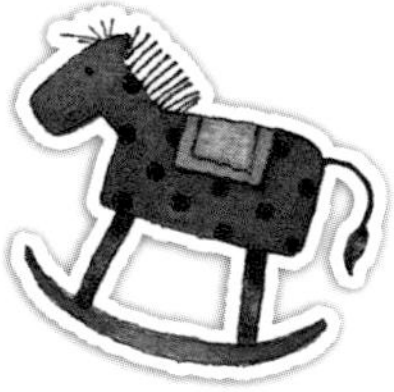

7. To two units from step 6, sew a 1½" x 10½" red ribbon piece. To the remaining two units, sew a 1½" x 10½" green ribbon piece. Press. Make two of each.

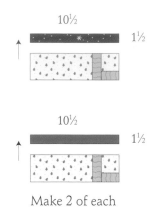

10½

1½

10½

1½

Make 2 of each

8. Sew a 10½" x 7½" background piece to each unit from step 7. Press. Make two of each.

7½

10½

7½

10½

Make 2 of each

9. Sew a 1½" gold ribbon square between a 1½" x 3½" and a 1½" x 7½" red ribbon piece. Press. Make two. Sew a 1½" gold ribbon square between a 1½" x 3½" and 1½" x 7½" green ribbon piece Press. Make two of each.

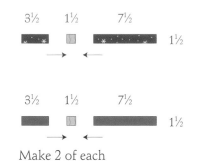

3½   1½   7½

1½

3½   1½   7½

1½

Make 2 of each

10. Sew two green strips from step 9 to the sides of two red units from step 8 as shown. Sew two red strips from step 9 to the top of two green units from step 8. Refer to diagram below for placement. Make two of each.

Make 2 of each

11. Sew unit from step 2 between two units from step 10, referring to the diagram for placement. Make two.

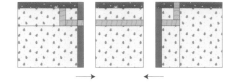

Make 2

12. Referring to diagram for placement, sew together two 8½" x 30½" outside border pieces, two 1½" x 30½" green ribbon strips, two units from step 11, and unit from step 4. Press.

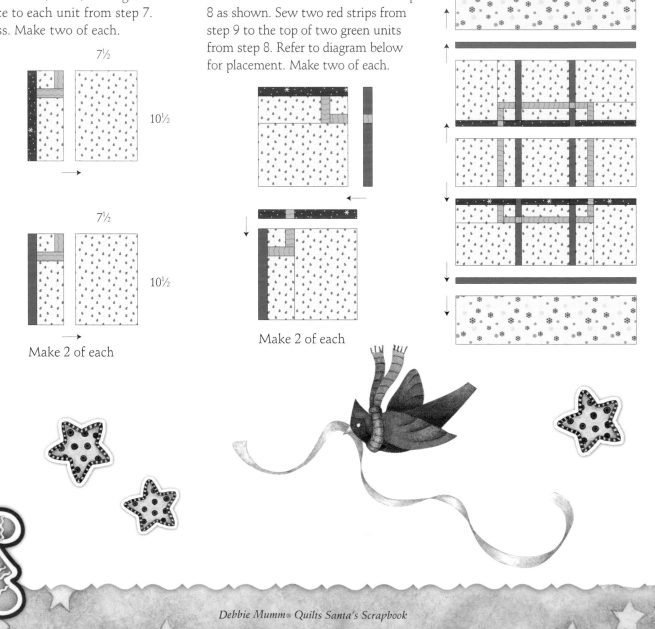

13. Sew one 1½" green ribbon square between one 1½" x 8½" and one 1½" x 39½" red ribbon piece. Press. Make two.

Make 2

14. Referring to diagram for placement, sew an 8½" x 30½" outside border piece between two 1½" x 8½" green ribbon pieces and two 8½" outside border squares. Press. Make two.

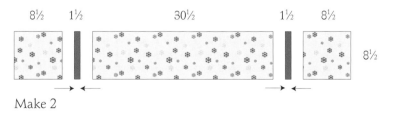

Make 2

15. Referring to quilt layout on page 56, sew center unit from step 12 between two units from step 13 and two units from step 14. Press. Appliqué holly in corners, if desired, from pattern on page 48.

Layering and Finishing

1. Cut backing fabric crosswise into two equal pieces. Sew pieces together to make one 56" x 84" (approximate) backing piece. Trim to 56" square. Arrange and baste backing, batting, and top together referring to Layering the Quilt directions on page 110.

2. Machine or hand quilt as desired.

3. Cut two binding strips in half and sew half to each of four remaining binding strips. Refer to Binding the Quilt directions on page 111 and use the pieced binding strips to bind the quilt.

59

Sweet Treats Apron

Fabric Requirements

Bib and neck ties - ½ yard
Waist ties - ½ yard
Waistband - ⅛ yard
Skirt - ½ yard
First, third, and fifth skirt
    borders - ⅛ yard
Second skirt border - ⅙ yard
Fourth skirt border - ⅛ yard
Pockets - ¼ yard
Pocket trim - Scrap
Lining - ⅞ yard
Lightweight Batting - 1⅛ yard
Holly leaf trim - Scrap
⅛" Black Cording - 1½ yards
Template plastic or paper
Lightweight fusible web
    ⅛ yard

Sweet Treats Apron
Photo Page 62

*This charming pinafore features faux lacing and contrast
quilting on the border. Your favorite cook will look wonderful
wearing this apron during the holidays. Use a decorative fabric
for the lining and the apron is reversible. Read all instructions
before beginning and use ¼"-wide seams throughout.*

60

Cutting the Strips and Pieces

Before you begin, read Cutting the Strips and Pieces on page 108.

		FIRST CUT		SECOND CUT	
		Number of Strips or Pieces	Dimensions	Number of Pieces	Dimensions
	BIB AND NECK TIES	1	11½" x 42"	2	11½" squares
		1	4½" x 42"	2	4½" x 15"
	WAIST TIES	2	6½" x 42"	2	6½" x 28"
	WAISTBAND/ LINING	1	2½" x 42"	2	2½" x 17½"
	SKIRT	1	17½" x 37"		
	FIRST, THIRD, AND FIFTH SKIRT BORDERS	2	1" x 42"	2	1" x 37"
		1	1½" x 42"	1	1½" x 37"
	SECOND SKIRT BORDER	1	4½" x 37"		
	FOURTH SKIRT BORDER	1	3½" x 37"		
	POCKETS	1	6¾" x 42"	4	6¾" x 7"
	POCKET TRIM	2	1¾" x 7"		
	LINING	1	26½" x 37"		

Making the Apron

1. For neck ties, with right sides together, fold 4½" x 15" strips in half lengthwise. Using ¼" seam allowance, stitch along one short end and the long edge. Clip corners, turn, and press. Make two.

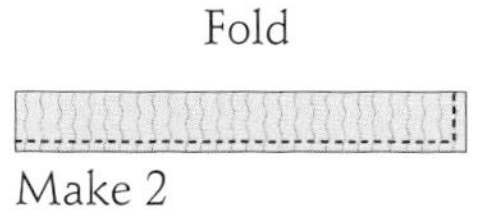

Fold

Make 2

2. To make apron bib, position two 11½" bib squares with right sides together. Insert unfinished ends of ties from step 1 between the two bib pieces with edges even at the top and ½" from the sides. Layer 11½" batting piece underneath. Stitch around sides and top. Trim corners and batting and turn right side out. Press. Topstitch if desired.

3. For waist ties, fold 6½" x 28" strips in half lengthwise with right sides together. Measure 3¼" from the bottom corner and make a mark. Draw a diagonal line from this point to the top corners to be used as a cutting line. Sew ¼" from raw edges and ¼" from drawn line at the ends.

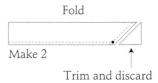

Fold

Make 2

Trim and discard

4. Trim ends ¼" from stitched line and turn ties right side out. Press.

5. With right sides together, position waist ties on waistband, making a small pleat in each tie allowing for a ¼" seam allowance on waistband. Baste. Center and pin bib to right side of waistband matching raw edges. Waistband will extend 3" on each side of bib.

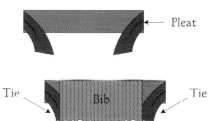

Pleat

Tie   Bib   Tie

6. On right side of waistband lining, press under ¼" along one long edge. Pin lining to waistband, bib, and ties with right sides together and matching raw edges. Beginning ¼" from bottom edge, stitch around sides and top with a ¼" seam. Clip corners, turn right side out, press, and set aside.

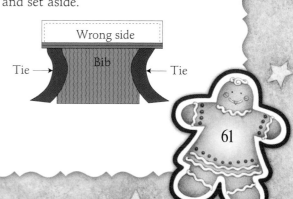

Wrong side

Tie   Bib   Tie

7. Before assembling skirt, baste a 4½" x 37" batting strip to the 4½" x 37" second skirt border strip. Then sew together the skirt, first, second, third, fourth, and fifth border strips as shown. Press.

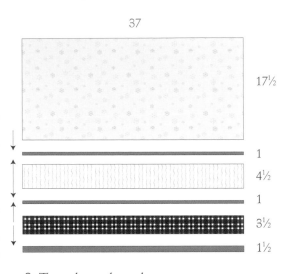

37

17½

1

4½

1

3½

1½

8. To make each pocket, sew one 1¾" x 7" pocket trim piece between two 6¾" x 7" pocket pieces. Press. Make two.

7   1¾   7

6¾

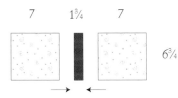

Make 2

9. Fold pocket in half right sides together. Trace pocket curve pattern on page 63 onto template plastic or paper and cut out. On the wrong side of outside corners of each pocket unit from step 8, trace around the curve template as shown and trim.

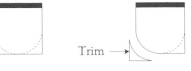

Trim →

10. Stitch pockets along sides and ¼" from drawn curved line, leaving a 3" opening on side for turning. Clip corners, turn, and press. Slipstitch pocket closed.

11. Trace holly pattern below, and add holly appliqués to pockets, referring to Quick-Fuse Appliqué directions on page 109. Refer to color photo on page 62 for placement on pocket.

12. Position pockets on skirt 6¼" inches from sides and 4½" inches from top. Edgestitch to skirt along sides and bottom.

13. Trace holly leaf quilting pattern from page 48 onto template plastic and trace onto second skirt border (with batting), referring to layout on page 60 for placement. Machine or hand quilt now or after apron is constructed.

14. To add lining to skirt, position skirt unit and 26 ½" x 37" lining piece with right sides together. Stitch along sides and bottom edge. Clip corners, turn, and press.

15. Baste across the top of apron skirt and lining and gather to fit waistband unit from step 6. With right sides together, pin waistband to skirt front, matching raw edges. Adjust gathers. Stitch ¼" from raw edges, being careful not to catch turned edge of waistband lining in the seam. Fold waistband to back and press. Slipstitch waistband lining to skirt lining.

16. To add cording, pin center of cord at bottom center of apron bib. Mark bib with chalk or pins ¾" on each side of center. Mark every 2½" to within 1" of top of bib. Refer to layout on page 60 and tack cording at marked points. Tie a bow at center top of bib and trim ends of cord. Hand or machine quilt apron bib with lattice pattern and skirt with holly pattern, if not previously quilted.

Apron front

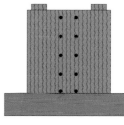

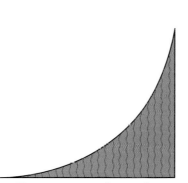

Curve to trace for pocket

Holly template for pocket

Warm and Spicy Gingerbread House

Warm & Spicy Gingerbread House
Finished size: 7½" x 8¾" x 5½"

Sugar and spice and everything nice describes this whimsical three-dimensional fabric gingerbread house. Use it to hold cookies or special treats on your table, or give as a treasured gift. Candy buttons and rickrack icing trim this delightful confection. Read all instructions before beginning and use ¼"-wide seams throughout.

Materials Needed

House - ⅝ yard brown fabric
House lining and pockets
  1 yard
Roof, lining, and pockets
  ½ yard
Upper House Accent - ⅙ yard
Windows, Door, and
  embellishments - Scraps
Candy-shaped Buttons - 41
  assorted (optional)
  (see Product Resource List,
  page 111)
Plastic canvas - Six sheets of
  10 mesh
¼"-wide Ribbon - 4 yards
Batting - 20½" x 26½" and
  7" x 12½" pieces
Fusible Web - ⅓ yard

Cutting the Strips and Pieces

Before you begin, read Cutting the Strips and Pieces on page 108.

		FIRST CUT		SECOND CUT	
		Number of Strips or Pieces	Dimensions	Number of Strips or Pieces	Dimensions
	HOUSE	1	18½" x 24½"		
	UPPER HOUSE ACCENT	2	5" x 9"		
	HOUSE LINING/ POCKETS	1	20½" x 42"	1	20½" x 26½"
				2	5¾" x 6"
		1	8½" x 42"	2	8" x 9¾"
	ROOF	1	12½" x 42"	2	7" x 12½"
				2	6¾" x 7"
	RIBBON	24	6" strips		

Making the House

1. On wrong side of the 18½" x 24½" house piece, measure, draw, and cut the outline of the house, using the diagram below as a measuring and cutting guide.

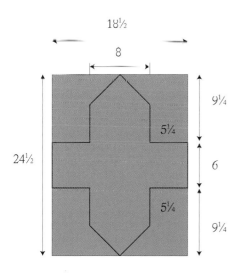

2. Refer to Quick-Fuse Appliqué directions on page 109. Trace upper house accent, window, and door appliqué designs from page 67. Fuse upper house appliqué. Fuse two windows and a door to the house front on the right side of the fabric.

Fuse two windows to back of house and one window to each side panel. Machine satin stitch or blanket stitch appliqué edges if you plan to wash the house.

3. Layer batting between wrong side of house fabric and lining. Stay stitch ⅛" from house raw edges as shown. Stitch along inside fold lines as shown.

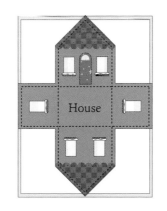

4. Trim batting and lining to the house raw edges. Quilt as desired.

5. Sew buttons and decorative trims as desired. Keep placement of buttons away from seam lines. **Option:** You may sew buttons after pockets are added, but you must be careful not to catch pockets with stitching. Add blanket stitch embroidery to upper house accent if desired.

Adding the Pockets

1. Double turn ¼" and stitch along one 6" side of two 5¾" x 6" pocket pieces. Repeat on one 8" side of each of the two 8" x 9¾" pocket pieces.

2. With right sides together, position and pin pocket pieces beneath four house side sections placing finished edges of pockets toward outside of house. Sew through the outside edges of house and pocket, pivoting at corners and using a ¼" seam. Trim excess fabric, turn, and press.

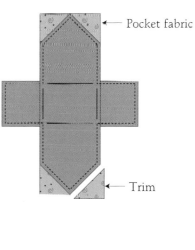
Pocket fabric

Trim

3. Cut a piece of plastic canvas slightly smaller than each pocket. Insert into pocket.

4. Hand stitch one end of 6" ribbon to pocket at each dot on diagram.

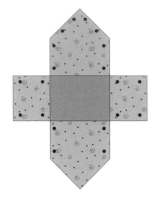

Adding the Roof

1. Place 7" x 12½" piece of batting between wrong sides of two 7" x 12½" roof pieces. Stay stitch ⅛" from raw edge on all sides and stitch down center seam.

12½

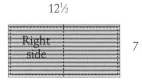

| Right side | | 7 |

2. Double turn ¼" and stitch along one 7" side of two 6¾" x 7" roof pocket pieces.

3. With right sides together, place roof pocket pieces on top of roof, matching outside raw edges and with hemmed edge near roof center. Stitch ¼" along all raw edges, clip corners, turn, and press. Stitch rickrack along edge of roof if desired. Hand sew one end of four 6" ribbon pieces where indicated to inside one half of roof.

4. Cut plastic canvas slightly smaller than roof pockets and insert in each.

Finishing

1. Cut a 5½" x 7½" piece of plastic canvas and place it inside the house for a base.

2. Tie ribbons together on the inside of the house, leaving one side of roof free of ribbon to allow easy access to goodies like our Gingerbread Cookie recipe on page 55!

Tracing Line —————————

Tracing Line - - - - - - - - -
(will be hidden behind other fabrics)

Starlight mint

Elf Tip

Debbie Mumm® candy-shaped buttons are available online at www.millhill.com or by calling (800) 356-9438. We used Starlight Mints #43163, Gumdrops #43160, Crossed Candy Canes #43164, and Hollyberry sets #43168. If desired, you can use appliqué templates on this page in place of the buttons.

Holly

Candycanes

Fold

Upper Accent House
Cut 2

Gumdrop

Snowflakes

Appliqué Door Pattern

Appliqué Window/ Window Box pattern

Cut 1

Cut 6

67

Gingerbread Garland

Gingerbread Garland
Finished size: 86" long

*Lovable gingerbread kids, miniature elf stockings, and
button candies team up on this winsome garland.
Gingerbread boys and girls are all dressed up
with vests, pinafores, and rickrack trim.
Gingerbread kids can also be used as tree ornaments.*

Materials Needed

Gingerbread boys and girls
 ¼ yard felt (72" wide) or
 ⅓ yard felt (36" wide)
Clothing - Colorful scraps
 and pieces
Elf Stockings - Colorful scraps
 and pieces
Cording - 2½ yards
Candy buttons - 6
 (see Product Resource List,
 page 111)
Assorted beads, buttons,
 embroidery floss, and trims
Heavyweight Fusible Web
 ⅓ yard
Template plastic

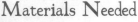

Making the Garland

1. Cut ten 5" x 6½" pieces of felt. Trace pattern for gingerbread boy and girl onto template plastic. Trace around template onto five pieces of felt, making three boys and two girls.

2. With wrong sides together, layer traced felt pieces from step 1 with remaining five felt pieces. Stitch on traced line. Cut about ¼" from stitched line with pinking shears.

Rickrack placement

Stitch line

Rickrack placement

Stitch line

3. Trace patterns for dress and vest onto paper side of fusible web. Referring to Quick-Fuse Appliqué directions on page 109, fuse clothing onto gingerbread kids.

4. Add beads for eyes, buttons to clothes, and embroider mouths using stem stitch (see Embroidery Stitch Guide on page 108).

5. To make elf stockings, refer to directions on pages 33-34.

6. Referring to the color photo for placement, position the gingerbread kids, stockings, and buttons along the cording, spacing them about 6" apart. Using clear, monofilament quilting thread, make a loop at the top of each felt figure and stitch to cording so they hang below the garland. Add stockings in the same manner. Sew buttons together in pairs. Tie a piece of clear thread between buttons and attach to cording.

69

Mrs. Claus' Christmas Project

Mrs. Claus' Christmas Project
Finished size: 54" x 66"
Photo Page 72

Rich velvets, warm wools, cozy flannels, and all your favorite fabrics combine to make this stunning "crazy quilt." We accented ours with hand and machine embroidery and a velveteen border trimmed with decorative braid. Read all instructions before beginning and use ¼"-wide seams throughout.

Fabric Requirements

Crazy Quilt Blocks - 5½ yards total (approximately) of assorted colorful scraps and pieces of velvet, wool, cotton, flannel, or satin

Foundation - 2¾ yards cotton cut into 20 pieces, 13" square

Accent Border - ¼ yard velveteen

Outside Border - ¾ yard velveteen

Binding - ⅔ yard velveteen

Backing - 3½ yards

Batting (optional) - 62" x 74" piece of lightweight batting or preshrunk flannel

Decorative braid or trim 7 yards (approximately)

Assorted decorative threads

Elf Tip

How about making this a group project? A crazy quilt is perfect for a group of people to join together and create. Each person can make one or more blocks from her own stash of special fabrics and add favorite hand or machine embroidery touches. When it's sewn together, it will be truly a one-of-a-kind treasure.

70

Making the Blocks

You will be making twenty Crazy Quilt Blocks and assembling them into rows. For each block, begin with a 13" foundation square and a center piece to use as a beginning point. Then add various shapes and fabrics to the beginning shape until your block is complete. Use as few or as many fabrics as you prefer. Our blocks are entirely scrappy. The yardage given is a generous estimate of a combination of over fifty fabrics.
Reminder: when adding velvet pieces, finger press only.

Our blocks have an average of 17 pieces consisting of 3 velvets, 5 wools, 6 cottons, 2 flannels, and 1 satin. Add machine or hand embroidery, or other embellishments to the blocks. Refer to page 108 for Embroidery Stitch Guide. Trim blocks to 12½" square.

Option: For a quick trick to speed up your Crazy Quilt piecing, try sewing several smaller pieces together before you add it to your foundation. Once you've sewn several of your favorites together, add it to your block as one piece.

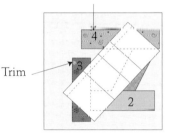

Piece before adding

1. Trace around the Crazy Quilt template on page 73 to make a pattern for your beginning or center shape. Pin the pattern to fabric, cut out, and position with right side up near the center of a 13" foundation square. We used mostly pentagon shapes (as the template indicates), but you can also use triangles and squares. If you use the same shape template throughout, your blocks can be very different, especially if the blocks are turned in different directions.

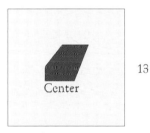

13

13

Center

Foundation

2. With right sides together, place the next piece of fabric on the center piece, making sure that edge of piece 1 is even with the edge of center piece as shown. Stitch ¼" from edge of piece 1 and flip right side up. Press as needed, but finger press only when using velvet.

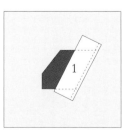

3. With right sides together, position piece 2 with center edge and stitch. Trim excess fabric from piece 1 if it will lie under piece 2. Press.

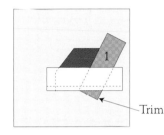

Trim

4. Continue adding pieces until foundation fabric is covered. Press or finger press.

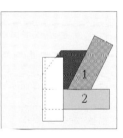

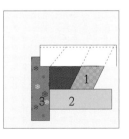

5. Repeat to make twenty blocks. Have fun making each of them look unique as you use different colors, fabrics, and sizes of pieces.

Elf Tip
Don't forget your walking foot! When you work with lovely, textural fabrics like velvet or satin, it will help to hold them in place as you sew. Also, anytime you're using a foundation fabric your walking foot is a great tool to use.

71

Cutting the Strips and Pieces

Before you begin, read Cutting the Strips and Pieces on page 108.

		FIRST CUT	
		Number of Pieces	Dimensions
	ACCENT BORDER	7	1" x 42"
	BORDER	7	3" x 42"
	BINDING	6	2³/₄" x 42"

Assembly

1. Arrange blocks into five rows of four blocks each, adjusting until you are pleased with the arrangement. Stitch rows together and join rows. Press.

2. Sew together two accent border strips end to end. Repeat for two more accent border strips. Repeat to sew together two sets of outside border strips. Set these four pieced strips aside.

3. Cut one accent border strip in half crosswise and sew each half to a remaining accent border strip. Repeat for outside border strips.

4. Sew a short accent border strip lengthwise to each short outside border strip. Repeat for each long accent border strip and long outside border strip.

5. Measure quilt through center from side to side and add 8". Trim short border units to this measurement. Repeat for long border units, measuring through center of quilt from top to bottom and adding 8."

6. Referring to Mitered Borders directions on page 110, sew mitered borders on the quilt.

7. Arrange and baste backing, flannel or batting (optional), and top together referring to Layering the Quilt directions on page 110.

8. Quilt in the ditch between blocks and in the borders as desired. Quilt may also be tacked or tied.

9. Hand or machine stitch decorative braid on outside border ¼" from inside seam if desired.

10. Sew two binding strips together end-to-end in pairs. Cut one binding strip in half and sew a half to each remaining binding strip. Referring to Binding the Quilt on page 111, add binding to the quilt.

72

Crazy Quilt template

Embossing Velvet

To add even more interest to our crazy quilt, we embossed some of our velvet pieces. Embossing velvet is easy using a rubber stamp and your iron. Look for a rubber stamp designed for printing on fabric. These generally have deeper, bolder lines. Avoid stamps with shallow cuts and lots of detail. Be sure the stamp you select can withstand heat from an iron.

1. Preheat iron to a dry setting between wool and cotton.

2. Position velvet square face down on the rubber stamp in desired position. Mist lightly with water.

3. Press with iron for 20 to 30 seconds and lift iron straight up from fabric. Do not slide! You will see the design on the wrong side. Lift velvet away from stamp to see the embossing on right side.

Gift Ideas

You can use the crazy quilt technique to make a wide variety of gifts and home accessories. Here are just a few ideas:

1. Use your crazy quilt blocks to make the Turned-up Toes Stockings on page 36. Or, just make the stocking cuff using the crazy quilt technique.

2. Use the crazy quilt method to make the front for a vest. Use velvet, velveteen, or silk for the back and be sure to line the vest so your seams won't show!

3. Add a sumptuous fringe and make your crazy quilt blocks into charming accent pillows.

4. An antique chair deserves a covering from the Victorian tradition. Make your crazy quilt blocks large enough to completely cover your chair cushion and wrap around underneath.

5. Use five of our 12" square blocks to make an unusual table runner. Add borders to complement your home décor.

6. We chose a traditional color palette for our crazy quilt, but you could also select pastels for a totally different look. How about a baby quilt in pastel colored cottons?

73

Reindeer Games

Santa's Reindeer

Deer Feed

Santa's
reindeer
leap so high
While intricate snowflakes
drop from the sky,
And when the deer land
with a joyful bound
They leave tiny hoof prints
on the ground.

Let it Snow Wall Quilt

Let It Snow Wall Quilt

Finished Size: 32" x 32"
Photo: page 78

Fabric Requirements

Fabric A Snowflake - ¾ yard
Fabric B Background - ¾ yard
Accent Border - ¼ yard
Outside Border - ⅓ yard
Corner Diamonds - ¼ yard
Binding - ⅜ yard
Backing - 38" square
Batting - 38" square
Heavyweight fusible web
   1 yard
Template Plastic
Appliqué scissors or craft knife
Marking pen with fine point

A wondrous snowflake of leaping stags and trees forms the center of this elegant wallhanging. The octagonal shape accentuates the snowflake design. Four layers are cut at once on the snowflake to make cutting easy, and the snowflake is quick-fused to the background. A template is provided for the diamonds on the border. This project is easier than it looks and the unique shape and motif will make this wallhanging a stunning focal point in your holiday decorating. Read all instructions before beginning and use ¼"-wide seams throughout.

Cutting the Strips and Pieces

Before you begin, read Cutting the Strips and Pieces on page 108.

		FIRST CUT		SECOND CUT	
		Number of Strips or Pieces	Dimensions	Number of Pieces	Dimensions
☐	FABRIC A	1	24½" square		
⬛	FABRIC B	1	24½" square *		
▨	ACCENT BORDER	4	1¾" x 42"	4	1¾" x 11" **
				4	1¾" x 15" **
⬛	OUTSIDE BORDER	3	2¾" x 42"	8	2¾" x 12⅛"
▨	CORNER DIAMONDS	2	2¾" x 42"		
▨	BINDING	4	2¾" x 42"		

*Tip: It is extremely important that you cut the square accurately.
  Draw square on wrong side of fabric to make sure angles are accurate.
**Mitered Accent Border requires eight 1¾" x 12½" strips.

Preparing the Center

Using see-through ruler and soft-leaded pencil, measure 7⅛" on each side of the four corners of Fabric B Background Square and make a pencil mark. Draw a diagonal line from the marks at each side of the corners as shown. Cut along this line at each corner to make center background.

Adding the Borders

1. When sewing border strips, always place octagon underneath with border piece on top to prevent stretching. Sew one 1¾" x 11" accent border strip to each of four opposite sides of background. Press and trim corners of each accent strip, using remaining sides as trimming guide as shown.

2. Add 1¾" x 15" accent borders to remaining sides, using adjoining sides as trimming guide. Press.

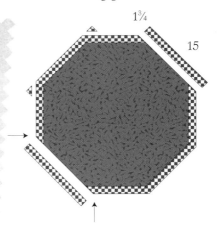

3. Using four 2¾" x 12⅛" outside border strips, repeat step 1 to add outside borders to four opposite sides.

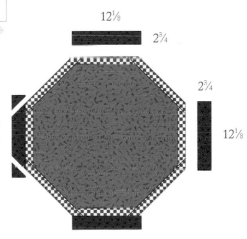

4. Trace corner diamond template onto template plastic and cut out. Trace and cut eight diamonds from two 2¾" x 42" corner diamond strips.

5. To prepare remaining 2¾" x 12⅛" outside border strips, measure and mark from each end of a long side of remaining four border strips using diamond template guide. Draw a diagonal line. Cut along this line.

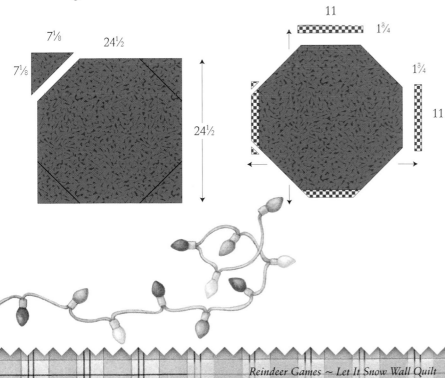

6. Sew diamonds to each end of remaining four border strips as shown. Press.

2¾

Make 4

7. Sew units from Step 6 to remaining sides of background octagon.

Adding the Snowflake

1. Trace snowflake pattern onto template plastic and cut out.

2. Following manufacturer's instructions, iron heavy-weight fusible web to the wrong side of 24½" Fabric A square.

3. With right sides together, fold the Fabric A square from step 2 diagonally. Fold again as shown.

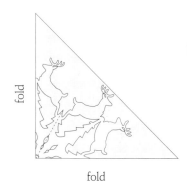

fold

fold

4. Trace snowflake template on the paper side of folded square, referring to diagram above. You will draw around the template three times, flipping as shown.

5. With fine-point appliqué scissors or craft knife, cut out the snowflake. You will be cutting through four layers.

6. Remove paper from the back of snowflake design and place fabric in the center of quilt. Consult layout on page 76 for proper positioning. After it is correctly positioned, fuse with iron, following manufacturer's directions.

Layering and Finishing

1. Arrange and baste backing, batting, and top together, referring to Layering the Quilt directions on page 110.

2. Machine or hand quilt as desired.

3. Fold four 2¾" x 42" binding strips in half lengthwise and press. Matching raw edges, sew binding strips to quilt top on four opposite sides. Trim along quilt edge. Repeat on remaining four sides, trim ½" from each edge to allow for turning raw edges to the inside when hand stitching.

Cutting Tip

We cut out the finely detailed antlers last. First we cut all four layers of the head and "rough cut" around the antlers. Then we cut the antlers one layer at a time, cutting the first layer and lining up the head on the second layer. After redrawing around the antlers we cut them out, then repeated the process for the last two layers.

78

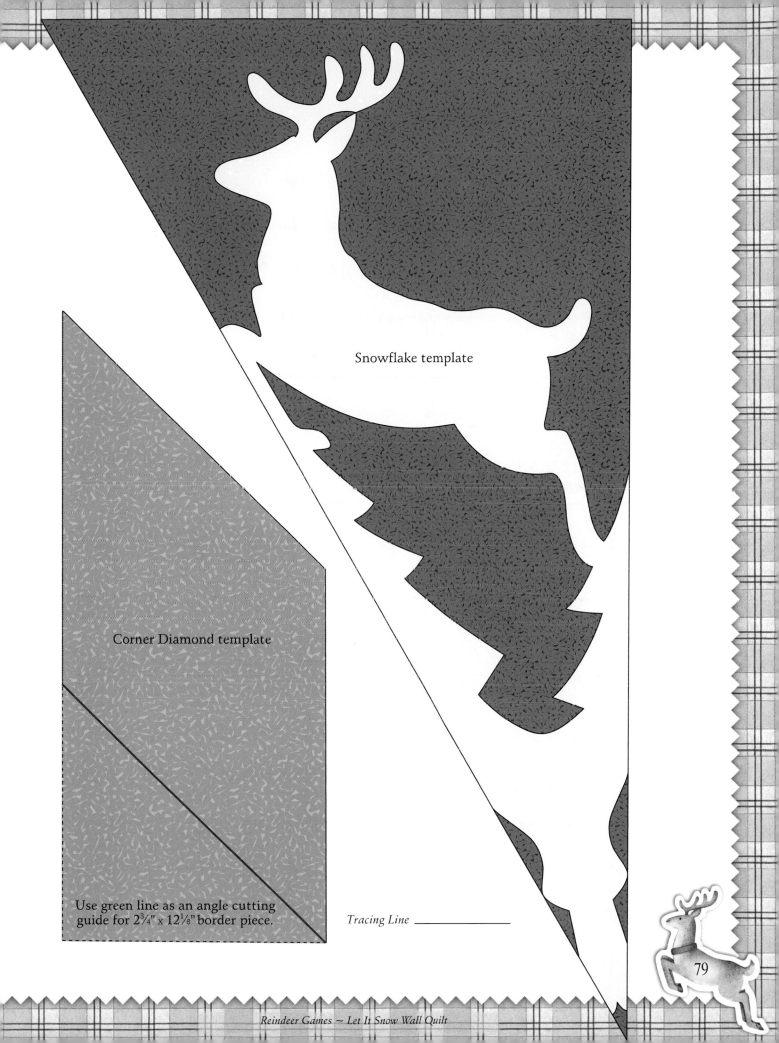

Snowflake template

Corner Diamond template

Use green line as an angle cutting guide for 2¾" x 12⅛" border piece.

Tracing Line _____

Leap for Joy Quilt

Leap for Joy Quilt

Finished Quilt Size: 78" x 105"
Photo page 82

Six stags leap across this spectacular bed-size quilt that is suitable for any time of the year. The background is easily pieced and the stags are machine appliquéd for durability. Read all instructions before beginning and use 1/4"-wide seams throughout.

Fabric Requirements

Fabric A (Background) - 4 yards
Fabric B (Triangles/Squares) 1/2 yard
Fabric C (Squares) - 1/4 yard
Fabric D (Triangles) - 1/3 yard
Fabric E (Block 1 Triangles) 7/8 yard
Fabric F (Block 2 Triangles) 7/8 yard
Fabric G (Block 1 and 2 First Accent Border) - 2/3 yard
Fabric H (Block 1 Second Accent Border) - 3/8 yard
Fabric I (Block 2 Second Accent Border) - 3/8 yard
Fabric J (Large Square) - 5/8 yard
Fabric K (Block Border) 2/3 yard
Fabric L (Block 1 Deer) 1 1/2 yards
Fabric M (Block 2 Deer) 1 1/2 yards
Inside Border - 5/8 yard
Middle Border - 3/8 yard
Outside Border - 1 3/4 yards
Backing - 6 1/2 yards
Binding - 7/8 yard
Batting - 86" x 113" piece
Lightweight fusible web 2 1/2 yards
Template Plastic

80

Cutting the Strips and Pieces

Before you begin, read Cutting the Strips and Pieces on page 108.

		FIRST CUT		SECOND CUT	
		Number of Strips or Pieces	Dimensions	Number of Pieces	Dimensions
	FABRIC A	6	22½" x 42"	6	22½" squares
	FABRIC B	3	3½" x 42"	24	3½" squares
		2	3" x 42"	24	3" squares
	FABRIC C	2	3" x 42"	24	3" squares
	FABRIC D	3	3½" x 42"	24	3½" squares
	FABRIC E	4	3½" x 42"	12	3½" squares
				12	3½" x 6½"
		4	3" x 42"	48	3" squares
	FABRIC F	4	3½" x 42"	12	3½" squares
				12	3½" x 6½"
		4	3" x 42"	48	3" squares
	FABRIC G	12	1¾" x 42"		
	FABRIC H	6	1¾" x 42"		
	FABRIC I	6	1¾" x 42"		
	FABRIC J	6	3" x 42"	24	3" x 5½"
				20	3" squares
	FABRIC K	7	3" x 42"	20	3" x 11½"
BORDERS					
	INSIDE	8	2½" x 42"		
	MIDDLE	8	1½" x 42"		
	OUTSIDE	9	6½" x 42"		
	BINDING	10	2¾" x 42"		

Making the Blocks

You will be making six deer blocks, three of Block 1 and three of Block 2. Each finished block measures 27½" square. After assembling the blocks and adding borders, appliqué the deer to the block centers.

Block 1 (Make three)

1. For Block 1, sew twelve 3½" Fabric B squares to twelve 3½" Fabric D squares, referring to Quick Corner Triangle directions on page 108. Make twelve.

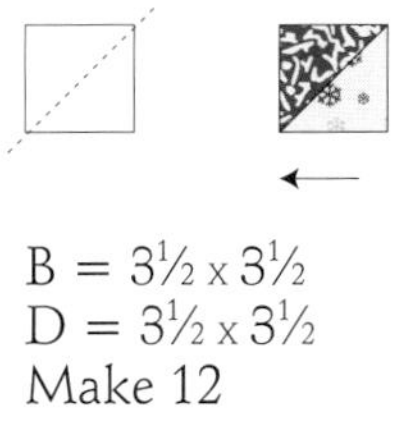

B = 3½ x 3½
D = 3½ x 3½
Make 12

2. Sew a 3½" Fabric E square to each unit from step 1. Make twelve.

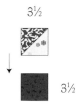

3½

3½

Make 12

3. Sew a 3½" x 6½" Fabric E piece to each unit from step 2 as shown. Make twelve.

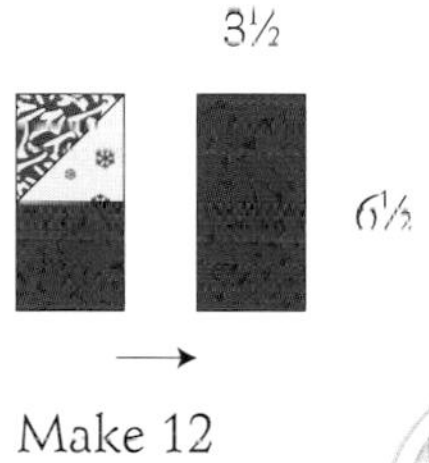

3½

6½

Make 12

4. With right sides together, position one unit from step 3 as shown at each corner of 22½" Fabric A background square. Draw a diagonal line from corner to corner as shown. Stitch along drawn line. Trim seam to ¼" and press. Repeat to make three.

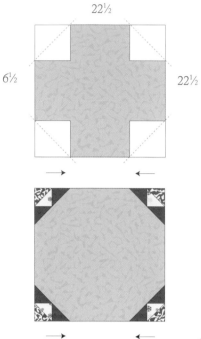

Make 3

5. Referring to Quick Corner Triangle directions on page 108, sew two 3" Fabric E squares to one 3" x 5½" Fabric J piece. Press. Repeat to make twelve.

E = 3 x 3
J = 3 x 5½
Make 12

6. Sew six 1¾" x 42" Fabric G strips and six 1¾" x 42" Fabric H strips together lengthwise in pairs. Press. Cut into twenty-four 3" x 9" segments.

Cut 24

7. Referring to Quick Corner Triangle directions on page 108, sew a 3" Fabric E square to one end of each of twelve units from step 6. Press. Repeat sewing twelve Fabric E squares to opposite end of each remaining twelve units.

E = 3 x 3

Make 12

E = 3 x 3

Make 12

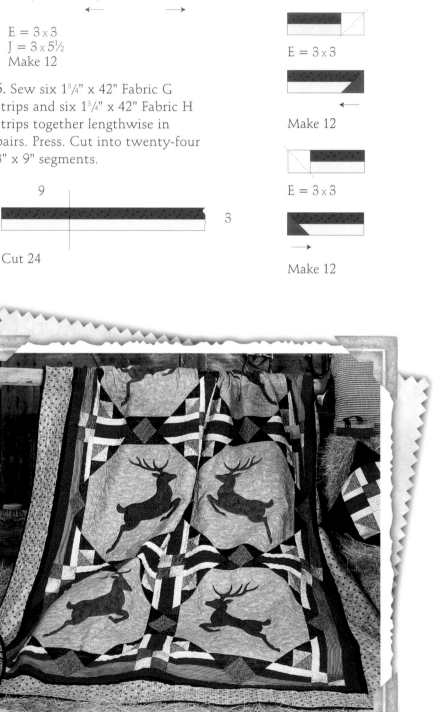

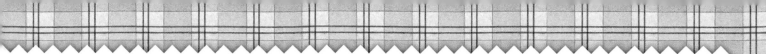

8. Sew each unit from step 5 between two units from step 7, referring to the diagram for placement. Press. Make twelve sets.

Make 12

9. Sew unit from step 4 between two units from step 8. Repeat to make three. Press.

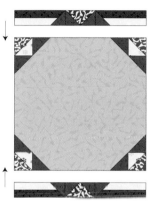

Make 3

10. Sew a 3" Fabric C square to each end of six units from step 8. Press

11. Sew units from step 10 to sides of Block 1 from step 9. Press. Block will measure 27½".

Block 1

Block 2 (Make three)

1. Repeat steps 1-11 above to make Block 2. Substitute triangle Fabric F (for Fabric E) in steps 2, 3, 5, and 7; and second accent border Fabric I (for Fabric H) in step 6; and Fabric B (for Fabric C) in step 10.

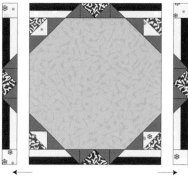

Block 2

Assembly

1. Refer to quilt layout on page 80 and assemble quilt in three rows with two blocks in each row, alternating Blocks 1 and Blocks 2 as shown.

2. Sew a 3" Fabric J square on one end of each of ten 3" x 11½" Fabric K pieces, referring to Quick Corner Triangle directions on page 108. Repeat sewing remaining ten Fabric J squares to opposite end of each remaining Fabric K pieces.

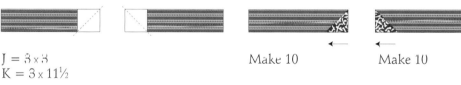

J = 3 x 3
K = 3 x 11½

Make 10   Make 10

3. Join units from step 2 together in pairs as shown, positioning units with triangles joining in the middle. Press. Make ten.

Make 10

4. Sew ten 3" Fabric C squares and ten 3" Fabric B squares together in pairs. Press.

5. Referring to diagram for placement, sew a unit from step 4 between two units from step 3 and one 3" Fabric B square and one 3" Fabric C square. Press. Repeat to make one each.

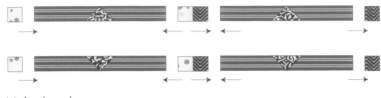

Make 1 each

6. Referring to diagram for placement, sew together three units from step 3, and four units from step 4. Press. Make one each.

Make 1 each

7. Referring to layout on page 80, sew units from step 5 to top and bottom of quilt and units from step 6 to sides.

Adding the Borders

1. Sew eight 2½" x 42" inside border strips together end to end in pairs. Referring to Adding Borders directions on page 110, sew inside borders to top and bottom of quilt and then to sides. Repeat to add middle border.

2. Sew eight 6½" x 42" outside border strips together end to end in pairs. Cut remaining strip in half and add one half to each of two pairs. Referring to Adding the Borders directions on page 110, sew borders to top and bottom and then to sides.

Adding the Deer

1. Trace deer pattern on pages 86-87 onto template plastic or paper and cut out.

2. Refer to Quick-Fuse Appliqué directions on page 109. Trace three appliqué designs in one direction on paper side of fusible web, then reverse template to trace additional three.

3. Fuse two left-facing deer and one right-facing deer to wrong side of Fabric L. Cut out on drawn line. Remove paper and fuse to Block 1.

4. Fuse two right-facing deer and one left-facing deer to wrong side of Fabric M. Cut out on drawn line. Remove paper and fuse to Block 2.

5. Machine appliqué around the edges of deer.

Elf Tip
To ensure consistent placement of deer, cut a large piece of tracing paper the size of background fabric. Place appliqué on paper in desired spot and trace. Use this paper as a template for proper placement.

84

Layering and Finishing

1. Cut backing fabric crosswise into two equal pieces. Sew pieces together to make one 84" x 117" piece. Arrange and baste backing, batting, and top together, referring to Layering the Quilt directions on page 110.

2. Machine or hand quilt as desired.

3. Sew ten 2¾" x 42" binding strips together end to end. Referring to Binding the Quilt directions on page 111, add the binding to the quilt.

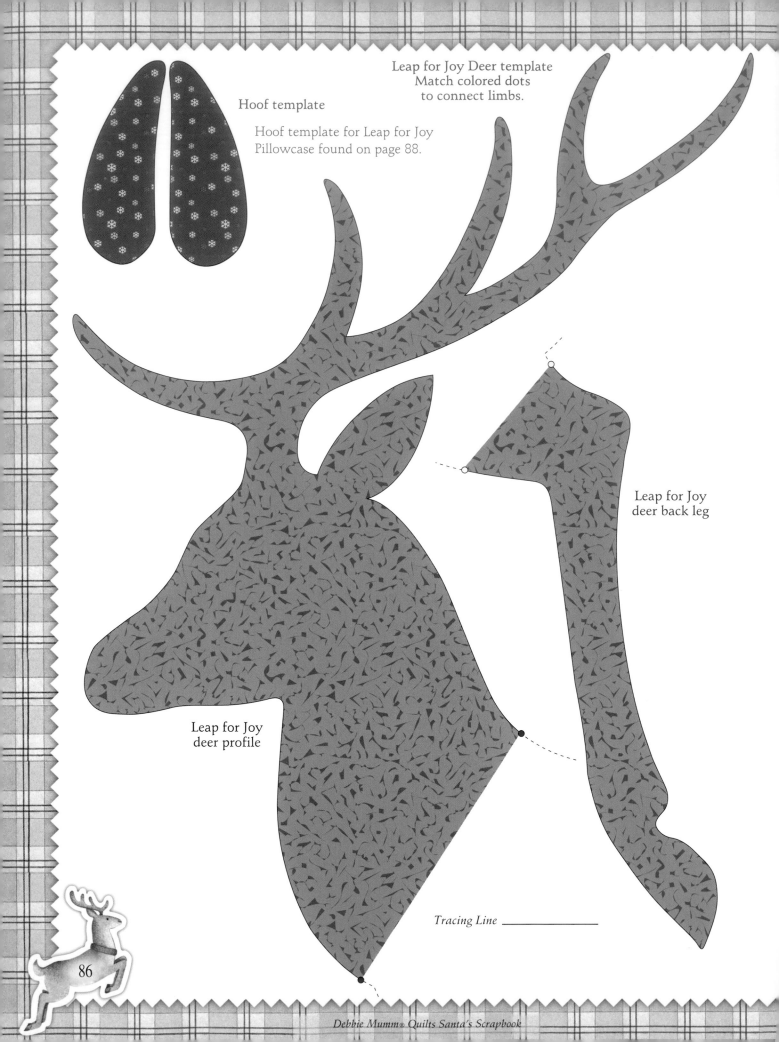

Hoof template

Hoof template for Leap for Joy
Pillowcase found on page 88.

Leap for Joy Deer template
Match colored dots
to connect limbs.

Leap for Joy
deer back leg

Leap for Joy
deer profile

Tracing Line _____

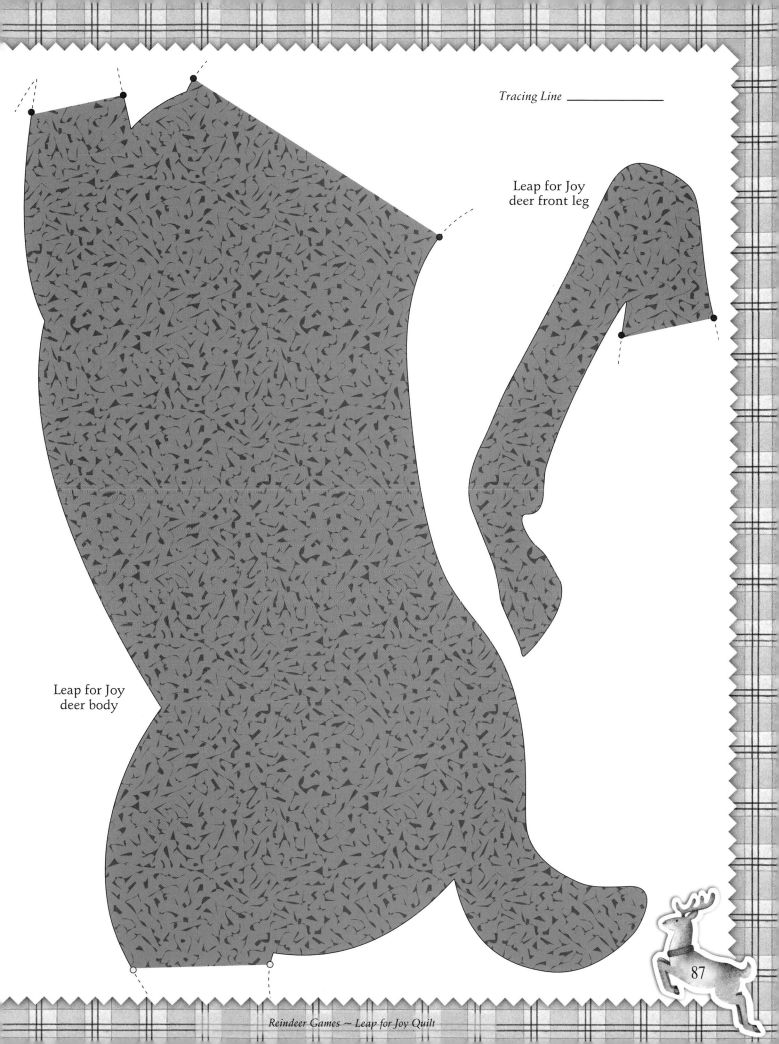

Tracing Line _____

Leap for Joy
deer front leg

Leap for Joy
deer body

87

Leap for Joy
Pillowcase & Accent Pillow

Leap for Joy Pillowcase and Accent Pillow

Finished Pillowcase Size: 30" x 20"
Finished Accent Pillow Size: 17" Square
Photo page 90

Tiny deer hoofprints land in the border of this pillowcase that matches our quilt. The rich colors of nature are highlighted by the striking border motif with its whimsical hoofprint. The bold piecing design of the Leap for Joy Quilt is set on point for the charming accent pillow. We also show you how to make a lap quilt using this easy pattern. Read all instructions completely before beginning and use 1/4"-wide seams throughout.

Fabric Requirements

Leap for Joy Pillowcase
For each pillowcase
Fabric A (Main Fabric)
    1¼ yards
Fabric B (Trim) - ⅛ yard
Fabric C (Triangles) - Scraps
Fabric D (Triangles) - Scraps
Fabric E (Center Square) - Scrap
Fabric F, G, and H (Strip Blocks)
    ⅛ yard of each
Fabric I (Backing and Lining
    Strip) - ⅝ yard
Hoofprints - Scrap (template on
    page 86)

Leap for Joy Accent Pillow
Fabric A (Four Patch Blocks and
    Triangles) - ⅙ yard
Fabric B (Four Patch Blocks)
    Scraps or ⅛ yard
Fabric C, D, and E (Strip Blocks)
    ⅛ yard of each
Fabric F (Triangles) - ⅛ yard
Fabric G (Corner Triangles)
    ⅜ yard
    Backing - ⅜ yard
    Lining - ½ yard
    Batting - 18" square
    Pillow Form - 16" square

LEAP FOR JOY PILLOWCASE

Cutting the Strips and Pieces

Before you begin, read Cutting the Strips and Pieces on page 108.
Makes one pillowcase

		FIRST CUT		SECOND CUT	
		Number of Strips or Pieces	Dimensions	Number of Pieces	Dimensions
	FABRIC A	2	20½" x 42"	2	23½" x 20½"
	FABRIC B	2	1" x 42"	2	1" x 20½"
	FABRIC C	4	3½" squares		
	FABRIC D	4	3½" squares		
	FABRIC E	1	6½" square		
	FABRIC F	1	2" x 42"	2	2" x 16"
	FABRIC G	1	2" x 42	1	2" x 16"
	FABRIC H	1	2" x 42"	1	2" x 16"
	FABRIC I	1	20½" x 42"	1	20½" x 14½"
				1	20½" x 7½"

Making the Borders

1. Referring to Quick Corner Triangle directions on page 108, sew one 3½" Fabric C square and one 3½" Fabric D square to opposite corners of 6½" Fabric E square. Repeat on remaining opposite corners.

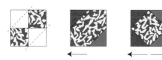

C = 3½ x 3½
D = 3½ x 3½
E = 6½ x 6½

2. Sew one each 2" x 16" Fabric G and H strips between two 2" x 16" Fabric F strips. Press. Cut into two 7½" x 6½" pieces.

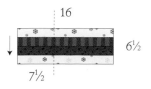

16

6½

7½

3. Sew one 3½" Fabric C square and one 3½" Fabric D square on the corners of units from step 2, referring to Quick Corner Triangle instructions on page 108. Repeat for remaining squares and remaining unit from step 2 except reverse the placement of the squares as shown.

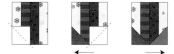

C = 3½ x 3½
D = 3½ x 3½

C = 3½ x 3½
D = 3½ x 3½

4. Sew triangle square unit from step 1 between units from step 3, matching Fabric C and Fabric D triangles in each unit. Press.

5. Add 1" Fabric B trim strips to each side and press.

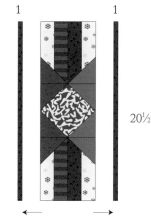

1   1

20½

6. With right sides together, sew 20½" x 7½" Fabric I piece to pieced border from step 5. Turn, press open.

7½

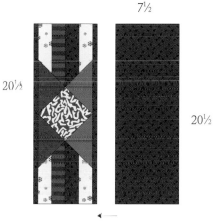

20½

20½

7. With right sides together, join pieced border unit from step 6 to 20½" x 14½" Fabric I piece by sewing together at both 14½" edges to form a loop. Press seams to one side.

8. Fold loop in half lengthwise, wrong sides together to form top edge of pillowcase.

9. With right sides together sew two 23½" x 20½" Fabric A pieces along three sides, leaving one 20½" edge open. Press.

10. Place unit from step 9 inside unit from step 8, right sides together matching raw edges. Stitch ¼" from edge. Zigzag or serge raw edge of seam to finish. Press. Appliqué hoofprint (pattern found on page 86).

89

LEAP FOR JOY ACCENT PILLOW
Cutting the Strips and Pieces
Before you begin, read Cutting the Strips and Pieces on page 108.

	FIRST CUT		SECOND CUT	
	Number of Strips or Pieces	Dimensions	Number of Pieces	Dimensions
FABRIC A	1	4" x 42"	4	4" squares
			2	3" squares
FABRIC B	2	3" squares		
FABRIC C	1	1¾" x 42"	2	1¾" x 20"
FABRIC D	1	1¾" x 42"	1	1¾" x 20"
FABRIC E	1	1¾" x 42"	1	1¾" x 20"
FABRIC F	1	4" x 42"	4	4" squares
FABRIC G	1	9⅜" x 42"	2	9⅜" squares *(cut once diagonally)*
BACKING	1	12" x 42"	2	12" x 17½"

Making the Center Block

1. Sew two 3" Fabric A squares and two 3" Fabric B squares together in pairs. Press. Sew the pairs together as shown to make Four Patch Block. Press.

2. Sew 1¾" x 20" Fabric D and Fabric E strips between two 1¾" x 20" Fabric C strips to make a strip set. Press. Cut strip set into four 4" segments.

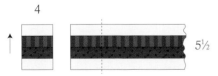

4

5½

3. Referring to Quick Corner Triangle directions on page 108, sew four 4" Fabric A squares to four 4" Fabric F squares. Press.

F = 4 x 4
A = 4 x 4
Make 4

4. Sew unit from step 2 between 2 units from step 3. Press. Make two.

Make 2

5. Sew unit from step 1 between 2 units from step 2. Press. Make one.

6. Sew unit from step 5 between two units from step 4. Press.

90

7. Sew two 9⅜" Fabric G corner triangles to two opposite sides of block. Press. Sew remaining two corner triangles to remaining two sides. Press.

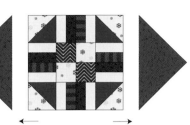

8. Layer batting between pillow top and lining. Baste. Hand or machine quilt as desired. Trim batting and lining even with raw edge of pillow top.

Finishing the Pillow

1. Narrow hem one long edge of each 12" x 17½" backing piece.

2. With right sides up, lay one backing piece over second piece so hemmed edges overlap. Baste pieces together at top and bottom where they overlap.

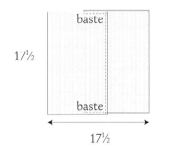

3. With right sides together, position and pin pillow top to backing. Sew around edges, trim corners, turn right side out, and press.

Just For Fun Lap Quilt

Finished Quilt Size: 45" x 62"

Fabric Requirements

Fabric A (Four Patch Blocks,
    Triangle Blocks) - ½ yard
Fabric B (Four Patch Blocks) - ⅛ yard
Fabric C (Strip Blocks) - ⅜ yard
Fabric D and E (Strip Blocks)
    ¼ yard each
Fabric F (Triangle Blocks) - ⅜ yard
Fabric G (Corner Triangles)
    ⅞ yard
Accent Border - ⅜ yard
Outside Border - ⅔ yard
Backing - 3 yards
Batting - 50" x 70" piece
Binding - ⅝ yard

Making the Blocks

1. Refer to the directions for Accent Pillow on pages 90 - 91. Follow steps 1 - 7 to make one block. Repeat for each of six blocks. Blocks measure 17½" square.

2. Sew six blocks together into three rows with two blocks in each as shown in quilt diagram.

Finishing the Quilt

1. Sew five 2" x 42" accent border strips end to end to make one continuous 2"-wide strip. Measure quilt through center side to side. Cut two 2"-wide accent border strips to that measurement. Sew to top and bottom. Press seam toward border strips.

2. Measure quilt through center from top to bottom, including borders just added. Cut two 2"-wide accent border strips to that measurement. Sew to sides. Press.

3. Repeat steps 1 and 2 to fit, trim, and sew five 4"-wide outside border strips to top, bottom, and sides of quilt.

4. Cut backing fabric crosswise into two equal pieces. Sew pieces together and trim to make one 53" x 70" (approximate) backing piece. Arrange and baste backing, batting, and top together, referring to Layering the Quilt directions on page 110.

5. Quilt as desired. Add binding to the sides, referring to Binding the Quilt directions on page 111.

And to All a Good Night

At
the end of
that wonderful
night so fair,
A tired Santa
returns to his slippers
and favorite chair.
He pulls out his scrapbook
and takes a look
At all the Christmases
past recorded in that book.

Starry Night Christmas Tree Skirt

Starry Night Christmas Tree Skirt

Finished size: 47" x 41"
Photo page 96

A beautiful star takes shape using a diamond log cabin variation
on this easy tree skirt. The rich colors and sophisticated design
will make this tree skirt a prized holiday tradition.
Read all instructions before beginning and use 1/4"-wide seams throughout.

Fabric Requirements
Star Block
Star center - ¹⁄₈ yard
Star Accent Border - ¹⁄₈ yard
Second Border - ¹⁄₃ yard
Third Border - ¹⁄₄ yard
Fourth Border - ¹⁄₃ yard

Background Block
Background - ¹⁄₂ yard
Accent Border - ¹⁄₄ yard
Outside Border - ¹⁄₂ yard

Backing - 2³⁄₄ yards
Batting - 45" x 51" piece
Binding - ¹⁄₂ yard

Cutting the Strips and Pieces

Before you begin, read Cutting the Strips and Pieces on page 108.

	FIRST CUT		SECOND CUT	
	Number of Strips or Pieces	Dimensions	Number of Pieces	Dimensions
▪ STAR CENTER	1	3½" x 42"	6	using diamond template
▨ STAR ACCENT BORDER	2	1½" x 42"		
▪ SECOND BORDER	3	3½" x 42"		
▪ THIRD BORDER	4	1½" x 42"		
▪ FOURTH BORDER	4	2½" x 42"		
▪ BACK-GROUND	2	6¾" x 42"	12	using triangle template
▪ ACCENT BORDER	4	1½" x 42"		
▫ OUTSIDE BORDER	4	3½" x 42"		
BINDING	6	2¾" x 42"		

Making the Blocks

You will be making six of the Star Block and twelve of the Background Block. The Star Block begins with a template piece and strips added to two sides form the points of the star. Refer to Assembly Line Piecing on page 108 to assemble Star Block. The Background Block also begins with a template shape and you will add borders to it. To make the tree skirt, assemble the completed blocks leaving one seam open.

Star Block (Make six)

1. Trace Star Block template on page 97 onto template plastic and cut out. Position template and cut out six times on 3½" x 42" star center strip.

2. Position and sew pieces from step 1 onto 1½" x 42" star accent border strip, referring to Assembly Line Piecing on page 108. Press. Trim following the diagonal line. Turn block and repeat to add remaining star accent border strip to adjacent side.

1½" Trim

1½"

3. Repeat step 2 using 3½" x 42" second border strips to add the second border to the same two sides. Refer to diagram for placement.

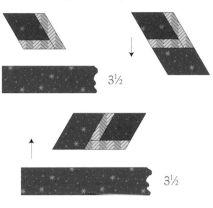

3½

3½

4. Repeat step 2 using 1½" x 42" third border strips to add the third border to the same sides.

5. Repeat step 2 using 2½" x 42" fourth border strips to add the fourth border to the same sides.

Background Block (Make twelve)

1. Trace background block template on page 97 onto template plastic and cut out. Position template onto two 6¾" x 42" background strips and cut to make twelve pieces.

2. Sew twelve pieces from step 1 onto 1½" x 42" background accent border strips, referring to Assembly Line Method directions on page 108. Press and trim using the sides of triangle pieces as a guide.

1½

Press 6 seams toward triangle and press 6 away from triangle.

95

3. Using 3½" x 42" outside border strips, repeat step 2 to add outside border. Make twelve.

3½

Press 6 seams toward triangle and press 6 away from triangle.

Assembly

1. Referring to diagram for placement, with right sides together, sew two Background Blocks to the side of Star Block. Press.

2. Repeat step to sew the remaining Background Blocks to the sides of remaining Star Blocks. Make 6.

Elf Tip
This pattern would make a beautiful table quilt. Just sew all seams and adjust your binding accordingly.

3. With Background Block edges positioned to the outside, sew three units from step 2 together to make half of the tree skirt. Press. Repeat to make the other half.

4. Sew two tree skirts halves from step 5 together, leaving one half of the seamed edge open to place around tree.

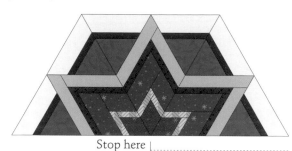

Stop here

Layering and Finishing

1. Arrange and baste backing, batting, and top together, referring to Layering the Quilt directions on page 110. Leave unsewn seam open.

2. Machine or hand quilt as desired.

3. Referring to Binding the Quilt on page 111, sew $2\frac{3}{4}$" x 42" binding strips end to end to make a continuous strip. Sew to every other side of quilt. Trim to edge. Continue sewing binding strips to remaining outside edges. Press binding away from quilt top. Trim, leaving extra $\frac{1}{2}$" for turning.

Background Block template

Grain of fabric

Star Block template

Grain of fabric

4. For center opening, press under the raw edge of one end of binding strip and place at center of quilt. Sew binding strip along one side. Trim, allowing $\frac{1}{2}$" extra to turn under.

5. Repeat for other side of center opening.

6. Fold binding to back of quilt and hand stitch.

And to All a Good Night Mantel Cover

And to All a Good Night Mantel Cover

Finished size: 44" x 16"
Photo page 100

A village sleeps under the night sky while lazy snowflakes drift to the ground. This delightful mantel cover or wall quilt uses easy piecing techniques for the houses. Appliqués, buttons, trims, and other embellishments add charming flourishes. Read all instructions before beginning and use 1/4"-wide seams throughout.

Fabric Requirements

Background & Prairie Points
   ⅞ yard
House Fronts - ⅛ yard each of
   five fabrics
Upper house, doors, windows,
   shutters, top trim, house
   base, roof, chimney -
   Assorted scraps
Trees - ¼ yard
Snow - ⅓ yard
Backing - 1⅓ yards
Batting - 48" x 20" piece
Ribbon - 1⅓ yards
Assorted buttons, beads,
   and trims

Elf Tip

To display your mantel cover, place four inches on the mantel and allow the rest to hang. You may set your decorations on top to hold the cover in place or secure with tape. Another option is to attach hook and loop tape on back at top edge and 2-3" away. Fasten tape together and insert a narrow rod or slat to secure.

98

Cutting the Strips and Pieces

Before you begin, read Cutting the Strips and Pieces on page 108.

	FIRST CUT		SECOND CUT	
	Number of Strips or Pieces	Dimensions	Number of Pieces	Dimensions
BACKGROUND	1	8½" x 42"	1	8½" x 30½"
	1	7½" x 42"	2	7½" x 16½"
	1	3½" x 42"	10	3½" squares
PRAIRIE POINTS	2	4" x 42"	17	4" squares
UPPER HOUSE	5	6½" x 3½" (five fabrics)		
HOUSE FRONT 1 AND 5	2	6½" x 2½"		
	2	2" square		
	2	1¾" x 3½"		
	2	1½" x 3½"		
	2	1" x 3½"		
HOUSE FRONT 2 AND 4	2	3" x 3½"		
	4	1¼" x 3½"		
	4	1½" squares		
HOUSE FRONT 3	1	6½" x 2½"		
	2	1¼" x 3½"		
	2	1" x 3½"		
	2	1½" x 1¾"		
DOORS 1 AND 5	2	2¼" x 3½"		
DOORS 2 AND 4	2	2" x 3"		
DOOR 3	1	2" x 3½"		
WINDOWS 1 AND 5	2	2" square		
WINDOWS 2 AND 4	4	1½" x 2½"		
WINDOW 3	2	1½" x 2¼"		
SHUTTERS 1 AND 5	4	1¼" x 2"		
SHUTTERS 4	4	1" x 2½"		
TOP TRIM 2 AND 4	2	6½" x 1"		
BOTTOM TRIM 2 AND 4	2	6½" x 2"		
SNOW	3	3" x 42"		
ROOFS	10	1¼" x 6"		
CHIMNEYS	2	1½" x 2"		

Making the Houses

You will be making five houses for your Village Mantel Cover. House 1 and House 5 are pieced the same but made from different fabrics and trims. House 2 and House 4 are pieced the same with appliquéd doors. House 3 is pieced. Roofs, shutters, chimneys, and some trims are appliquéd. Each finished house block measures 6½" x 8½".

House 1 and House 5

1. Referring to Quick Corner Triangle directions on page 108, sew two 3½" background squares to one 6½" x 3½" upper house piece.

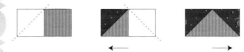

Upper House = 6½ x 3½
Background = 3½ x 3½

2. Sew 2¼" x 3½" door between 1" x 3½" and 1¾" x 3½" house front pieces. Press.

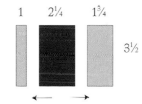

3. Sew 2" square window to 2" square house front piece. Press.

4. Sew unit from step 3 between unit from step 2 and a 1½" x 3½" house front piece. Press.

99

5. Sew a 6½" x 2½" house front piece to the unit from step 4. Press.

6. Sew upper house unit from step 1 to top of house front unit from step 5. Press seam down. House block measures 6½" x 8½". Repeat steps 1-6 to make House 5.

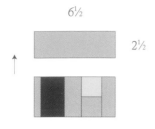

House 2 and House 4

1. Repeat step 1 for Houses 1 and 5 to make upper house unit.

2. Sew two 1½" x 2½" windows to two 1½" house front squares. Press.

3. Referring to diagram for placement, sew a 3" x 3½" house front piece between window units from step 2 and two 1¼" x 3½" house front pieces. Press.

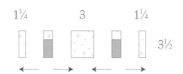

4. Sew unit from step 3 between a 6½" x 1" top trim piece and a 6½" x 2" bottom trim piece. Press.

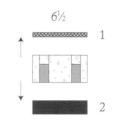

5. Sew upper house unit from step 1 to house unit from step 4. House block measures 6½" x 8½". Press seam up. Repeat steps 1-5 to make House 4.
Note: On House 2 we sewed trim above bottom trim piece.

House 3

1. Repeat step 1 for Houses 1 and 5 to make upper house.

2. Sew two 1½" x 2¼" windows to two 1½" x 1¾" house front pieces. Press.

3. Sew the 2" x 3½" door between two 1" x 3½" house front pieces. Press.

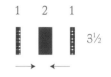

4. Sew door unit from step 3 between two window units from step 2. Press.

5. Sew door/window unit from step 4 between two 1¼" x 3½" house front pieces. Press.

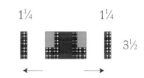

6. Add 6½" x 2½" house front piece to the top of unit from step 4. Press.

7. Sew upper house unit from step 1 to house unit from step 5. House block measures 6½" x 8½". Press seam down.

Assembly

1. Sew five house blocks together joining 8½" sides. Press.

2. Sew 8½" x 30½" background piece to top of house unit from step 1. Press. Add 7½" x 16½" background piece to each end. Press.

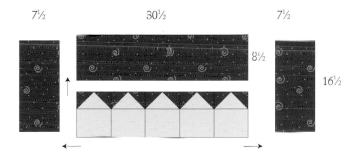

3. Referring to layout on page 98 and photo on page 100, press under seam allowances on roofs, shutters, doors 2 and 4, chimneys, and any trims you wish to add. Appliqué in place by machine or hand. The lower roof edges may be placed at the upper house edge or below—we varied the placement of ours.

4. To add snowdrift, first trace snow pattern from page 102 on freezer or tracing paper, connecting pieces A and B at dots. Trace three of piece AB onto freezer paper or template plastic. Cut one of piece C and one reversed. Join AB strips, then connect piece C at each end, overlapping to dotted line.

5. Sew three snow fabric strips together to make one long segment. Press. Fold fabric crosswise with right sides together. This will make the snow two layers thick which will prevent the darker fabrics underneath from showing through.

6. Place snow pattern on doubled fabric, aligning straight edge with bottom of strip. Trace curved line. Machine stitch on the line drawn. Trim seam to ¼" with pinking shears (if available). Turn right side out and press.

7. Place on top of mantel cover, aligning bottom edges. Snow will be slightly wider than mantel cover. Adjust to desired position and tack or appliqué in place. Refer to Appliqué directions on page 109.

8. Add trees to each end using quick fuse, machine, or hand appliqué. We finished our trees with blanket stitching in white to simulate snow. Refer to Embroidery Stitch Guide on page 108.

Finishing the Quilt

1. To make prairie points, fold and press 4" background squares in half diagonally and then in half again.

2. Position folded prairie points on snow, aligning with each end and matching raw edges with raw edges of mantel cover. Slide folded edges into open edges to overlap slightly. Baste in place.

3. Layer backing and mantel cover right sides together over batting. Using a ¼" seam allowance, stitch around edges leaving a 6" opening at the top. Trim batting and backing, turn and press. Press prairie points downward.

4. Slipstitch opening closed and quilt as desired.

5. Topstitch ribbon at intersection of prairie points and snow. Add other decorative trims, ribbons, embroidery, beads, and buttons as desired.

101

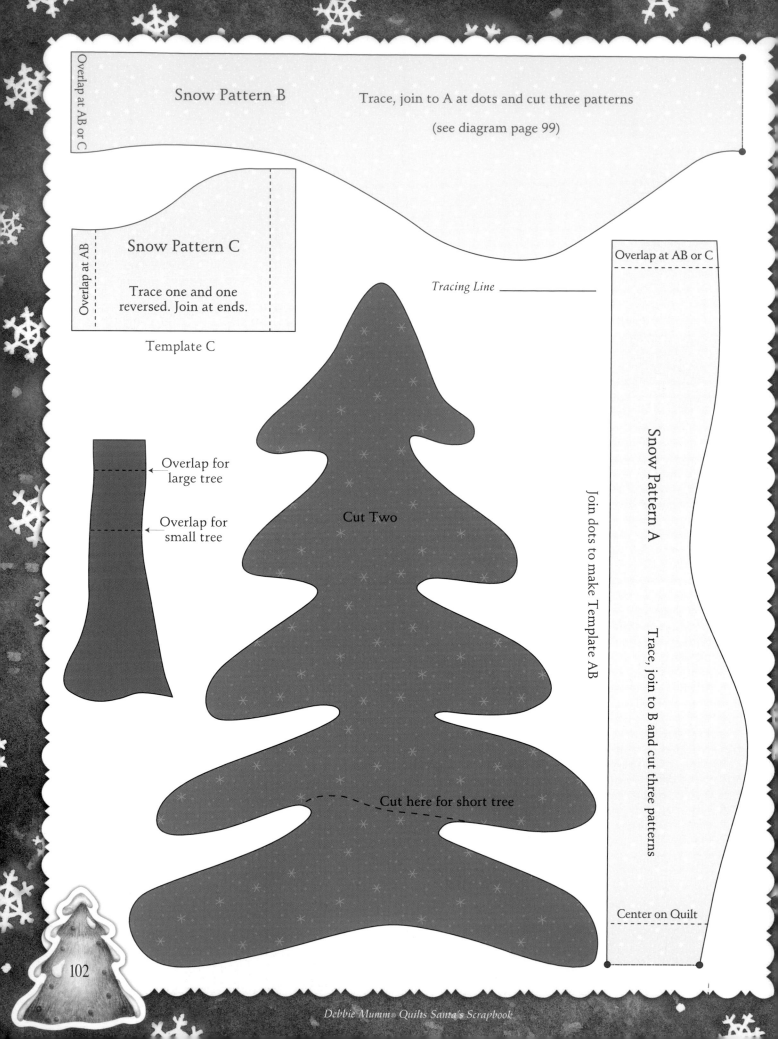

Snow Pattern B

Trace, join to A at dots and cut three patterns

(see diagram page 99)

Overlap at AB or C

Snow Pattern C

Overlap at AB

Trace one and one reversed. Join at ends.

Template C

Tracing Line _____

Overlap at AB or C

Cut Two

Overlap for large tree

Overlap for small tree

Snow Pattern A

Join dots to make Template AB

Trace, join to B and cut three patterns

Cut here for short tree

Center on Quilt

Snowflake Pattern

Sparkle Bright Snowflakes

Create the magical feeling of gently falling snow framed in windowpanes with these quick and easy snowflakes. These snowflakes would also look great on your Christmas tree!

Materials Needed

Ivory Craft Felt
Fusible Interfacing
Spray Adhesive
Crystal Glitter
Silver Thread

1. Trace snowflake patterns onto fusible interfacing.

2. Following manufacturer's directions, fuse interfacing to felt. The interfacing provides additional body to the felt.

3. Cut out snowflakes on drawn lines.

4. Spray one side of snowflake with adhesive and sprinkle with glitter. Let dry thoroughly, then repeat for the other side.

5. Use a silver thread to hang your snowflakes in the window or on your tree.

Snowflake Pattern

Santa's Scrapbook

Santa's Scrapbook

Treasure your memories with this heirloom-quality scrapbook.
A crazy quilt block embellished with embroidery personalizes the cover,
while velvet covers the back. Hints, tips, and ideas for creating your own
personalized scrapbook pages are also included.

Supplies Needed

Scrapbook - 12" or similar size that has a post-hinged binding (we used 12" x 12")

Crazy Quilt Block - square of foundation fabric 4" larger than scrapbook cover, decorative fabric scraps and trims (See Mrs. Claus' Christmas Project, page 70)

Lightweight Batting - ½ yard

Velvet - ½ yard for back cover

Lining - ½ yard for inside covers

Poster Board - Approximately 12" x 24"

Craft Knife

Fabric Glue

Spray Adhesive

Elf Tips

• *Be sure to use only archival-safe supplies to assemble your scrapbooks. Paper products should be both acid-free and lignin-free. To test the acidity of paper or memorabilia you plan to include in your scrapbook, use a pH pen.*

• *Deacidification spray can be used to preserve these paper keepsakes.*

Making the Cover

You will be making one Crazy Quilt Block for the front of your scrapbook. Refer to the instructions for Mrs. Claus's Christmas Project on page 71 to construct your crazy quilt block. The foundation of your block must be 4" larger than both dimensions of your purchased scrapbook cover.

Assembly

1. Remove the covers from the scrapbook and measure the width and length.

2. Cut two pieces of thin batting the size of these measurements. Glue them to the outside of the front and back covers.

3. Center the front cover of the scrapbook face down on the wrong side of the Crazy Quilt Block. You may want to use a spray adhesive to secure the block in place.

4. Fold corners of the Crazy Quilt Block diagonally over the corners of the scrapbook cover. Glue in place.

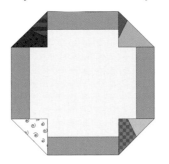

5. Beginning with opposite sides, fold edges of quilt block over edges of cover. Glue in place. Use a craft knife to cut small slits in the quilt block for the post binding.

6. Measure the inside of the front cover of the scrapbook from the front edge to the bend in the binding and top to bottom. Cut a piece of poster board that measures $3/8$" less than these measurements.

7. Cut a piece of lining fabric to the measurement in step 6 plus 2". Fold lining fabric over poster board, repeating the method from steps 4 and 5.

8. Position and glue wrong side of lining-covered poster board to inside of cover.

9. Repeat steps 4-8 to adhere velvet to the back cover and lining to inside back of scrapbook. Reassemble scrapbook.

Elf Tips

• *Use cookie cutters as templates to crop your photos. Or, use appliqué patterns from your quilt books! Try the snowflakes on page 103 or the gingerbread kids on page 69.*
• *Use alphabet stickers to title your pages*
• *Look at quilt patterns as inspiration for page layouts.*

Create Your Own Scrapbook Pages

1. Organize your photos. Sort them by person, by theme, chronologically, or however you anticipate compiling your scrapbooks.

2. Organize your memorabilia. Photos alone can't possibly tell the whole story! Include some of the precious artwork your children created that's hanging on your refrigerator, or how about some fabric from the stockings you stayed up so late to finish in time for Santa's visit?!

3. Choose a theme or style for your page(s). What do you want to emphasize in your photos? Study the photos and follow their lead for colors, actions, shapes, or patterns.

4. Experiment with different layouts. Plan to use 2 - 5 photos per page, to avoid a too-busy look.

5. Crop your photos using templates, a corner rounder, decorative edge scissors, or a shape silhouette.

6. Mount the cropped photo on coordinating acid-free paper, or frame it using a fun, coordinating paper or fabric scrap. Adhere photo layout on your scrapbook paper using an acid-free glue or adhesive.

7. Decorate your page with stickers that coordinate with your page's design elements. But be careful not to overdo it. You'll detract from the real focus of the page—your photos!

8. Be sure to record the facts pertaining to your photos on each page so that generations to come can relive the memories!

106

Elf Tip

Debbie Mumm® scrapbooks, papers, stickers, and supplies are manufactured by Creative Imaginations® and are available in stationery and scrapbooking stores. To locate a store near you, call Creative Imaginations at (800) 942-6487.

General Directions

Cutting the Strips and Pieces

Before you make each of the projects in this book, pre-wash and press the fabrics. Using rotary cutter, see-through ruler, and cutting mat, cut the strips and pieces for the project. If indicated on the Cutting Chart, some will need to be cut again into smaller strips and pieces. The approximate width of the fabric is 42". Measurements for all pieces include $\frac{1}{4}$"-wide seam allowance unless otherwise indicated. Press in the direction of the arrows.

Assembly Line Method

Whenever possible, use the assembly line method. Position pieces right sides together and line up next to sewing machine. Stitch first unit together, then continue sewing others without breaking threads. When all units are sewn, clip threads to separate. Press in direction of arrows.

Quick Corner Triangles

Quick corner triangles are formed by simply sewing fabric squares to other squares and rectangles. The directions and diagrams with each project show you what size pieces to use and where to place squares on corresponding piece. Follow steps 1–3 below to make corner triangle units.

1. With pencil and ruler, draw diagonal line on wrong side of fabric square that will form the triangle. See Diagram A. This will be your sewing line.

A.

sewing line

2. With right sides together, place square on corresponding piece. Matching raw edges, pin in place and sew ON drawn line. Trim off excess fabric leaving $\frac{1}{4}$" seam allowance as shown in Diagram B.

B.
trim $\frac{1}{4}$" away from sewing line

3. Press seam in direction of arrow as shown in step-by-step project diagram. Measure completed corner triangle unit to ensure greatest accuracy.

C.

finished corner triangle unit

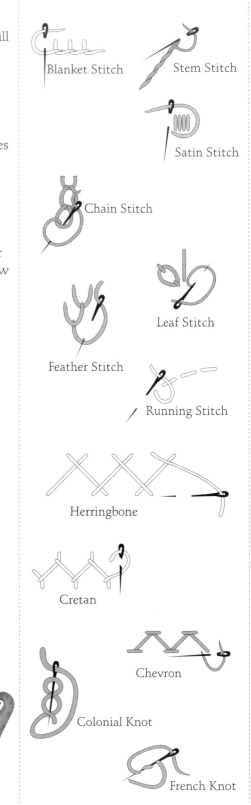

Embroidery Stitch Guide

Blanket Stitch

Stem Stitch

Satin Stitch

Chain Stitch

Leaf Stitch

Feather Stitch

Running Stitch

Herringbone

Cretan

Chevron

Colonial Knot

French Knot

Quick-Fuse Appliqué

Quick-fuse appliqué is a method of adhering appliqué pieces to a background with fusible web. For quick and easy results, simply quick-fuse appliqué pieces in place. Use sewable, lightweight fusible web for the projects in this book unless indicated otherwise. Finishing raw edges with stitching is desirable. Laundering is not recommended unless edges are finished.

1. With paper side up, lay fusible web over appliqué design. Leaving ½" space between pieces, trace all elements of design. Cut around traced pieces, approximately ¼" outside traced line.

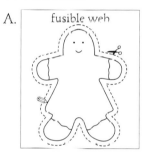

A. fusible web

2. With paper side up, position and iron fusible web to wrong side of selected fabrics. Follow manufacturer's directions for iron temperature and fusing time. Cut out each piece on traced line.

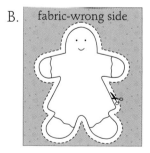

B. fabric-wrong side

3. Remove paper backing from pieces. A thin film will remain on wrong side. Position and fuse all pieces of one appliqué design at a time onto background, referring to color photos for placement.

Hand Appliqué

Hand appliqué is easy when you start out with the right supplies. Cotton or machine embroidery thread is easy to work with. Pick a color that matches the appliqué fabric as closely as possible. Use appliqué or silk pins for holding shapes in place, and a long, thin needle, like a sharp, for stitching.

1. Make a plastic template for every shape in the appliqué design. Use a dotted line to show where pieces overlap.

2. Place template on right side of appliqué fabric. Trace around template.

3. Cut out shapes ¼" beyond traced line.

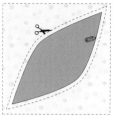

4. Position shapes on background fabric. For pieces that overlap, follow numbers on patterns. Pieces with lower numbers go underneath; pieces with higher numbers are layered on top. Pin shapes in place.

5. Stitch shapes in order following pattern numbers. Where shapes overlap, do not turn under and stitch edges of bottom pieces. Turn and stitch the edges of the piece on top.

6. Use the traced line as your turn-under guide. Entering from the wrong side of the appliqué shape, bring the needle up on the traced line. Using the tip of the needle, turn under the fabric along the traced line. Using blind stitch, stitch along the folded edge to join the appliqué shape to the background fabric. Turn under and stitch about ¼" at a time.

Machine Appliqué

This technique should be used when you are planning to launder quick-fuse projects. Several different stitches can be used; small narrow zigzag stitch, satin stitch, blanket stitch, or another decorative machine stitch. Use an appliqué foot if your machine has one. Use a tear-away stabilizer or water-soluble stabilizer to obtain even stitches and help prevent puckering. Always practice first to adjust your machine settings.

1. Fuse all pieces following Quick-Fuse Appliqué directions.

2. Cut a piece of stabilizer large enough to extend beyond the area you are stitching. Pin to the wrong side of fabric.

3. Select thread to match appliqué.

4. Following the order that appliqués were positioned, stitch along the edges of each section. Anchor beginning and ending stitches by tying off or stitching in place two or three times.

5. Complete all stitching, then remove stabilizers.

Adding the Borders

1. Measure quilt through the center from side to side. Trim two border strips to this measurement. Sew to top and bottom of quilt. Press toward border.

2. Measure quilt through the center from top to bottom, including the border added in step 1. Trim border strips to this measurement. Sew to sides and press. Repeat to add additional borders.

Mitered Borders

1. Cut the border strips as indicated for each quilt.

2. Measure each side of the quilt and mark center with a pin. Fold each border unit crosswise to find its midpoint and mark with a pin. Using the side measurements, measure out from the midpoint and place a pin to show where the edges of the quilt will be.

midpoint

3. Align a border unit to quilt. Pin at midpoints and pin-marked ends first, then along entire side, easing to fit if necessary.

4. Sew border to quilt, stopping and starting ¼" from pinmarked end points. Repeat to sew all four border units to quilt.

quilt front

5. Fold corner of quilt diagonally, right sides together, matching seams and borders. Place a long ruler along fold line extending across border. Draw a diagonal line across border from fold to edge of border. This is the stitching line. Starting at ¼" mark, stitch on drawn line. Check for squareness, then trim excess. Press seam open.

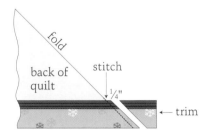

fold

back of quilt

stitch

¼"

trim

Layering the Quilt

1. Cut backing and batting 4" to 8" larger than quilt top.

2. Lay pressed backing on bottom (right side down), batting in middle, and pressed quilt top (right side up) on top. Make sure everything is centered and that backing and batting are flat. Backing and batting will extend beyond quilt top.

3. Begin basting in center and work toward outside edges. Baste vertically and horizontally, forming a 3"– 4" grid. Baste or pin completely around edge of quilt top. Quilt as desired. Remove basting.

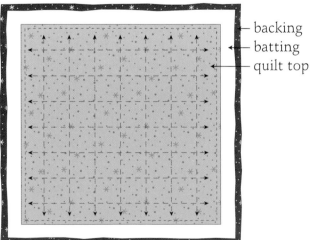

backing

batting

quilt top

Binding the Quilt

1. Trim batting and backing to ¼" from raw edge of quilt top.

2. Fold and press binding strips in half lengthwise with wrong sides together.

3. Lay binding strips on top and bottom edges of quilt top with raw edges of binding and quilt top aligned. Sew through all layers, ¼" from quilt edge. Press binding away from quilt top. Trim excess length of binding.

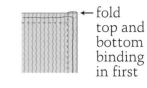

4. Sew remaining two binding strips to quilt sides. Press and trim excess length.

5. Folding top and bottom first, fold binding around to back then repeat with sides. Press and pin in position. Hand stitch binding in place.

← fold top and bottom binding in first

Product Resource List

To locate retail outlets for Debbie Mumm® products used in this book, please contact the following:

Fabric - South Sea Imports, (800) 829-0066, Fax (310) 763-4777, www.southseaimports.com.

Buttons - Mill Hill / Gay Bowles Sales, Inc. (800) 356-9438, www.millhill.com.

Scrapbook Supplies - Creative Imaginations, (800) 942-6487, Fax (714) 995-3213.

Dinnerware and Collectible Mini Teapots - Sakura Inc./Oneida, Ltd., (212) 683-4000, Fax (212) 683-4071.

Wallpaper - Imperial Home Décor Group, (800) 539-5399, Fax (800) 444-7865, www.imp-wall.com.

Wrapping Paper - Glitterwrap, (973) 625-4200, Fax (973) 625-9641 www.glitterwrap.com.

Stamps - Stampington & Company, (877) 782-6737, Fax (949) 380-9355, www.stampington.com.

To order a Debbie Mumm Catalog, please call (888) 819-2923 or (509) 466-3572 or visit our website at **www.debbiemumm.com**.

Discover More From Debbie Mumm®

Here's a sampling of some of the many other quilting and home décor books by Debbie Mumm. These books and specially designed patterns are available at your local quilt shop or by calling (888) 819-2923, or shop on-line at **www.debbiemumm.com**. When you order a Debbie Mumm® book, you'll receive a complimentary catalog filled with Debbie's most recent books, patterns, and selected gifts.

*Debbie Mumm's®
Birdhouses for every Season*
112-page, soft cover

*Debbie Mumm's®
12 Days of Christmas*
140-page, soft cover

*Debbie Mumm's®
Country Settings*
112-page, soft cover

*Debbie Mumm's
Project Kids™*
64-page, soft cover

Woodland Christmas
80-page, soft cover

Cottage In Bloom
40-page, soft cover

Winter Birds
pattern

Guardian Angel
pattern

Peace Quilt
pattern

1116 E. Westview Ct.,
Spokane, WA 99218
(509) 466-3572

Toll Free (888) 819-2923
Fax (509) 466-6919

www.debbiemumm.com

CREDITS

Designs by Debbie Mumm®
Special thanks to my creative teams:

EDITORIAL & PROJECT DESIGN
Carolyn Ogden: Managing Editor
Laura M. Reinstatler: Technical Editor
Pam Mostek: Writer
Maggie Bullock: Copy Editor
Georgie Gerl: Quilt and Craft Designer
Carolyn Lowe: Quilt and Craft Designer
Jackie Saling: Craft Designer
Kris Clifford: Scrapbook Designer
Candy Huddleston: Seamstress
Nancy Kirkland: Seamstress
Wanda Jeffries: Machine Quilter
Pam Clarke: Machine Quilter

BOOK DESIGN & PRODUCTION
Mya Brooks: Production Director
Tom Harlow: Graphics Manager
Sherry Hassel: Sr. Graphic Designer
Heather Hughes: Graphic Designer
Nancy Hanlon: Graphic Designer
Robert Fitzner: Graphic Designer

PHOTOGRAPHY
Peter Hassel Photography
Quad/Photo

ART TEAM
Lou McKee: Senior Artist
Kathy Arbuckle
Sandy Ayars
Heather Butler
Gil-Jin Foster
Kathy Riedinger

MARKETING & P.R.
Barbara Reinhardt: Director of
Sales and Marketing

Special thanks to Ted and Carolyn Lowe for providing the 1898 cabin for the location photography and to Melba and John Buck for lending the sleigh.

©2001 Mumm's The Word®, Inc.
Printed in the USA

Every attempt has been made to provide clear, concise, and accurate instructions. We used quick cutting and sewing methods most appropriate for you to successfully complete these projects. Other techniques may also achieve the same results.

All rights reserved. No part of this book may be photocopied or reproduced without written consent from Mumm's The Word®, Inc. All finished items produced from this book are protected by Federal Copyright Laws and may not be reproduced for commercial use in any form whatsoever without the express written consent of Mumm's The Word®, Inc.